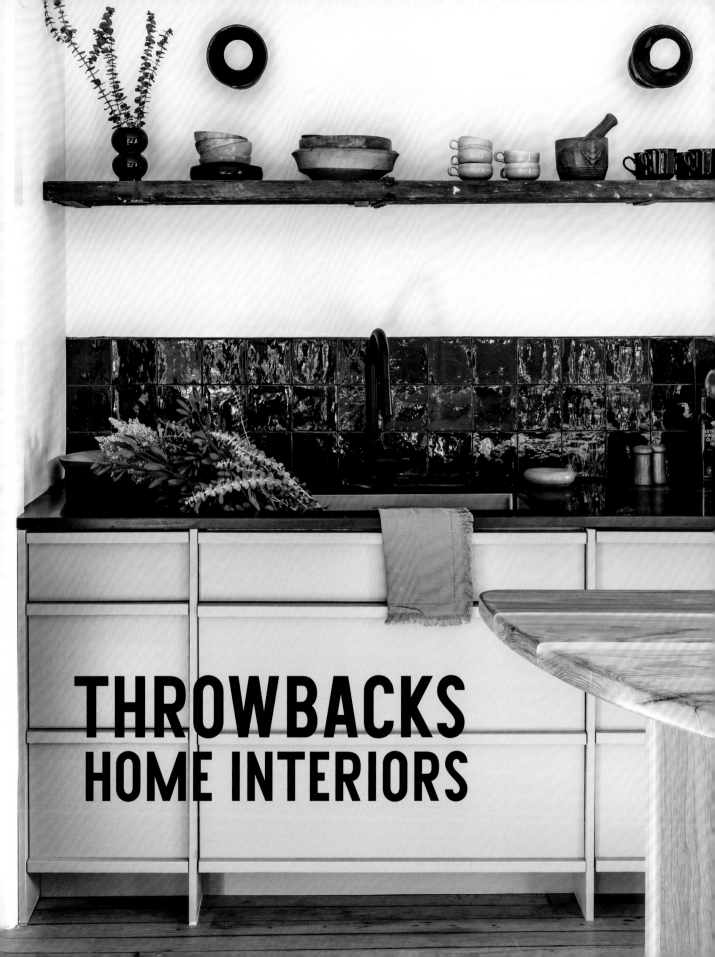

THROWBACKS
HOME INTERIORS

THROWBACKS
HOME INTERIORS

ONE OF A KIND HOME DESIGN FROM RECLAIMED & SALVAGED GOODS

BO SHEPHERD & KYLE DUBAY

WITH MEGAN ANDERLUH

PHOTOGRAPHS BY GERARD + BELEVENDER

CLARKSON POTTER/PUBLISHERS
NEW YORK

CONTENTS

INTRO

You never know when a seemingly mundane moment is going to change your life forever. Believe it or not, we can trace the beginning of our adventure to one object, found on the side of a Detroit street.

It's 2013. We're biking around the East Riverfront neighborhood, in the shadow of the city's oddest skyscraper, the Renaissance Center, which looks straight out of a sci-fi movie. A lot of industries used to collide here when the city was at its peak: coal from the south; copper, iron, and lumber from the north; and auto products made right in Detroit. But on that day, the paint on the brick warehouses was chipping, and many of the panes in the milky blue windows were empty. The summer weeds are growing up to our eyeballs.

Even though we're so close to downtown, we're pretty much the only ones around. Instead of other people, we're running into heaps of stuff piled all over the street. Unfortunately, this was a common sight around this time. Detroit was still reeling from the financial crisis, which had hit the city hard. People fell behind on rent or left for somewhere else, and landlords and contractors were responding by throwing the things they didn't take with them out on the curb.

Not everyone would find much to look at in this picture. But in Detroit, the more you look, the more you see—and what you see is often beautiful.

At some point, Kyle slows his bike. He says something along the lines of, "Whoa whoa whoa— what's *this*?" He's spotted a loveseat, a little worse for wear, but with ornately carved wooden legs and armrests. It's such an unexpected find among the clothes, bins, and trash bags—an object with a story: the life it had before us, how it got here, and now, how we had found it.

That loveseat—which we turned into a chair that still sits on our porch in Detroit's Corktown neighborhood—became Woodward Throwbacks' first salvage job.

We're Bo Shepherd and Kyle Dubay, and we founded our reclaimed furniture and design company, Woodward Throwbacks, to give a new story to the stuff we saw getting thrown away. We don't pick things up off the street much anymore, though we'll still pull the truck over if we see something really cool. After more than a decade of making the highest-quality reclaimed furniture and cultivating strong relationships in the city we call home, we're now privileged to be invited to salvage from some of Detroit's most remarkable spaces, from nineteenth-century mansions to automotive plants to old schools and churches.

Those aimless bike rides around the city have turned into a thriving business, with a full staff operating out of a 24,000-square-foot former auto dealership we turned into our warehouse, and a bright and shiny storefront in beautiful downtown Detroit. These days, we're working away on everything from finding and reclaiming special antiques, to building one-of-a-kind furniture from salvaged materials, to designing

interiors filled with the texture of objects that have a story.

We've learned a lot along the way—about history, creativity, sustainability, thrift, and hard work—and we want to share it with you. Over a decade of building a business, honing our craft, and diving deep into salvage and sustainable design, we've come to see our environment with new eyes, and we want this book to change how you see your world, too. This might mean learning how to incorporate a hand-me-down into your home in a way that feels exciting instead of boring. It might mean trusting yourself to buy that weird old couch at the flea market just because you love it, and experimenting with building your space around those quirky antique and salvage finds. Or it might mean seeing that heavy box of tile the previous owner left behind in your new basement as your next home-reno project rather than a chore.

As Woodward Throwbacks has grown, we've found a community of like-minded Detroit creatives, salvage junkies, and design nerds who have created homes that surprise, challenge, and inspire us. This book will take you on an exclusive tour of these Throwbacks Homes to show you the endless variety, imagination, and beauty that can result when you use antiques and reclaimed materials to make your house into a home. To us, the houses featured here aren't just remarkable spaces; we're talking about a way of living. There's built-in resourcefulness, originality, sustainability, and cost savings in creating your home from what you can find close at hand.

SO COME ON IN TO THESE THROWBACKS HOMES. WE COULDN'T BE HAPPIER YOU'RE HERE.

WHO WE ARE

WE'VE FOUND THERE ARE TWO KINDS OF PEOPLE: people who like brand-new stuff, and people who like stuff with history. At Woodward Throwbacks, we definitely fall into that second category. We're all about texture and imperfections, marks that give things character and tell you where they came from.

We're not sure where this love of old stuff started—no one is necessarily born a dumpster diver or antique picker. But growing up in Saginaw, Michigan, Kyle saw how his mom kept an eye out for any treasures that may have been put on the curb. And Bo learned from her dad that doing things right often meant doing things the hard way, watching him pull nails out of old wood boards so they could be reused to upgrade her childhood homes in New Jersey and Jamaica.

We also both liked to make things—Kyle in woodshop and odd jobs through high school and college, Bo through the budding car designer career that brought her to Detroit. Woodward Throwbacks really got started when we met here.

THROWBACK TO THE BEGINNING

The two of us met at a neighborhood cleanup sometime in 2013. We both were fascinated by Detroit's landscape, the empty buildings and lots, the beauty and history, the culture and community. So began the bike rides around the city that eventually started our business, since they often ended with us poking around piles of trash looking for treasures.

The neighborhood we lived in at the time, Brush Park, was particularly weird. Only a couple

of buildings survived of what used to be Detroit's Millionaire's Row, and these amazing Victorian mansions were either falling apart or just starting to be fixed up by people who saw a brighter future for the neighborhood. This meant contractors and demo crews were throwing away beautiful old-growth pieces of floor and trim.

We were young and creative and hated to see beautiful materials thrown away, so we decided to start making things: the construction waste became our own personal lumber supply. We started making the kind of home decor that we'd want to buy, mostly salvaged wood signs screen-printed with cheeky messages like "do epic shit" and "take your top off" (that last note appeared on a wall-mounted bottle opener).

We were operating out of garages and basements with extremely minimal supplies—a portable table saw, a chop saw. Eventually, we applied for a vendor spot at Eastern Market—Detroit's historic farmers market, where people have been selling everything from feed hay to flowers since the 1890s—and things started to take off. When we got our first wholesale order, it was time to get legit.

TRADING SPACES

The first Woodward Throwbacks space was a 3,000-square-foot, Art Deco brick building a few miles down Michigan Avenue from the bustling Corktown neighborhood. But by the time we fixed up the building and opened it to the public, we'd already outgrown it.

In the midst of renovating our new storefront and setting up shop, a customer asked us if we sold

The Home Base's sunroom is our favorite place in the house to hang out in the summer. When Covid was at its height, we gave it a facelift using almost as many reclaimed and found materials as possible.

THE METROPOLITAN
THEMETROPOLITANDETROIT.COM
WELCOME TO DETROIT
"THE MOST MISERABLE CITY IN AMERICA"
– FORBES MAGAZINE
INSIDE | Miserable Stories, About Miserable People, Living Miserable Lives... & Sudoku!

reclaimed materials—in addition to the small items and signs we were making at the time. We loved the idea, but the building didn't have the space. And Detroit real estate was heating up; if we waited too long, we might not be able to buy a bigger place.

After a little searching, we found our perfect site: a (wait for it) 24,000-square-foot former car dealership, with a showroom, offices, a workshop, and tons of storage space. It was located in Hamtramck, technically a separate city within the limits of Detroit, with the motto "the world in two square miles." Many of our neighbors have Polish, Yemini, or Bangladeshi roots, which means the food in our hood is fire and we're endlessly inspired by all the cultures around us.

When we say we were learning on the job, we're not exaggerating. We were outfitting our workshop with tools we found at garage sales or on Facebook Marketplace, and constantly calling in friends and connections for favors. We were learning how much it costs to operate a growing business, and to sell using traffic to Instagram as well as foot traffic. At one point, we were renting

out our house and living in the warehouse to make ends meet.

In short, we hustled, and ended up gaining loyal clients as well as national attention, and partnering with some cool brands. Our hard work was paying off. But much like the ever-changing city our business was inspired by, we always had our eye on what was next.

MOVING ON UP

The growth of Woodward Throwbacks has always been super organic—a mixture of the materials we had on hand; the spaces, skills, and equipment we had to work with; and sometimes, just getting bored and wanting to try something new. Once the warehouse gave us more room to store and experiment with the stuff we salvaged, we learned that most customers wanted polished, finished products rather than raw ingredients. So we started to make unique furniture out of reclaimed materials—often with clean, mid-century designs, but with the signature, impossible-to-replicate texture that

tells the story of what each piece is made of. As we got more practice and more tools, we leaned into creating lines of furniture that really allowed us to develop and refine our process.

These days, we're still thinking big, and getting excited about designing whole spaces as well as the stuff that goes in them. Our warehouse is still located in Hamtramck, but we've opened a storefront in the heart of downtown that allows us to bring our work to an even bigger audience. And we've started working on exciting interior design projects around the city, some of which appear in this book. Up next: converting an old warehouse in the Islandview neighborhood into our dream home.

Woodward Throwbacks is a perfect storm of working our asses off, blind optimism, risk-taking, resilience, sheer willpower, and some things just breaking the right way for us. When it comes down to it, we love what we do, and we've always just tried to read the room and seize opportunities when they appear. That's basically salvage in a nutshell.

We've learned a few things building our brand. We know how to work our way around antique shops, salvage yards, and yard sales, and we'd love to help you develop your very own picker's eye. We know how to style the hell out of a room using salvage, and think we can help you with that as well. And we also know how to build cool stuff, so DIYers should find something here, too. We can't wait to share what we've learned through the home tours in this book.

TALKING ABOUT SALVAGE

You hear a lot of words when you start to learn about salvage—*reclaimed*, *restored*, *refinished*, *repurposed*, *recycled*, *upcycled*, *antique*, *thrifted*, *vintage*, *DIY* . . . just to name a few. We use these terms and techniques all the time, and we don't care too much about getting them exactly right: for the most part, we're just learning as we go. But before we go any further, we do want to get a few things straight.

First, let's talk about preservation. This is the art of keeping something exactly the way it was when it was made, or restoring it to look like it did when it was brand spankin' new. Preservation is connected to terms like *restored*, *refinished*, and

Grandma's Touch of Soul

BAR·B·Q RIBS

RIB Tip Dinner

Hamburgers

CHILI dogs .99

20 pc. JUMBO SHRIMP with FRIES 14.9

SOUL FOOD $5.9

SUNDAY · all DINNERS

antique, words often used to describe something pristine and authentic to the time it was made.

We meet a lot of people who think of us as preservationists, but that's not how we see ourselves. We have a lot of respect for preservation, but it's usually too late to take the materials and objects we use back to the beginning. And honestly, that isn't what we're interested in. Salvaged materials come with all the texture, marks, and blemishes of a life well lived, and we wouldn't have it any other way.

Instead, we think of what we do as *adaptive reuse.* Since we often gravitate toward things that have been through too much to be perfectly restored, we feel free to re-envision what they could be. This philosophy goes for everything from our furniture—turning old signs into cabinet doors, or science lab tables into kitchen islands—to the buildings we've invested in: an auto repair shop becomes our warehouse; an industrial building becomes our future home.

Because adaptive reuse doesn't ask for perfection, it feels more sustainable and accessible. It's a way of honoring parts, pieces, and moments of history, while also acknowledging that we live in the twenty-first century and that convenience and

functionality are key. This balance between past and future is what Woodward Throwbacks is all about.

THE STORY BEHIND THE NAME

Around the time our reclaimed signs were selling like hotcakes in Eastern Market, it became clear that this could be a business, and that it needed a name. We liked "Woodward" because Woodward Avenue is Detroit's main drag, stretching all the way from the downtown riverfront to Eight Mile (the city limit) and beyond, and because it had "wood," the material we use the most, right in the name. "Throwbacks" maybe isn't as straightforward.

We didn't want to use words like *woodworking* or *antiques.* From the beginning, we thought of the business as a brand and a concept, and we didn't want to pigeonhole ourselves as just one thing, like furniture manufacturers or vintage resellers. "Throwbacks" isn't *vintage* or *antique*; it's a very nineties term for a blast from the past, and we're both nineties kids at heart. Irreverent, shouting out Detroit, nodding to the past: Woodward Throwbacks worked. The name stuck.

THE BASIC RULES OF SALVAGING

MOST OF THE BEAUTIFUL STUFF YOU'LL SEE decorating the homes in this book is secondhand, found everywhere from garage sales to antique stores; in some very special houses featured here, nothing at all was bought new. So we thought it might be helpful to give you some tips for making the perfect find whenever you're out salvaging—that is, antiquing, thrifting, whatever you'd like to call it.

The thing is, picking is an art. Whether you're searching on the curb or on Craigslist, the true rules of salvaging are that there are no rules—a good find depends on luck, keeping your eyes open, and trusting your gut. There are some things that salvage isn't, such as letting yourself into an abandoned building and having a free-for-all. We're proud to be welcomed into the spaces we salvage from by trusted community members, and when opportunities to do so are few and far between, there's always antique fairs, garage sales, Facebook Marketplace . . . the list goes on.

We have several strategies between the two of us when it comes to salvaging—game plans that usually complement, but sometimes straight up work against, each other. But that's how the magic happens. Here are some of the general guidelines we follow when we're going picking.

GO IN WITH A PLAN (JUST BE PREPARED TO DITCH IT).

Have you ever gone to the grocery store without a list and ended up with a bunch of stuff you didn't need, and nothing to make for dinner? Salvaging can be the same way. It's always good to have a running inventory of objects you've been looking for to guide you while you shop—like a specific chair for a special corner, or antique frames to fill out your gallery wall.

Kyle definitely salvages with a plan. He looks around purposefully and often goes right to the seller to ask for specific items. Bo's strategy is where the second part of this rule comes in.

Have you ever gone to the grocery store looking for a very specific item and gotten so caught up in the hunt that half an hour later, you haven't found anything on your list? Salvaging can be like that, too. If you're too focused on one thing, you might be blind to all the other cool stuff around you.

Bo tends to move more slowly when she's picking, allowing her attention to wander to whatever catches her eye. Sure, sometimes that means we lose track of what we were looking for in the first place and come home with something we absolutely can't use. But we've happened upon some of our best finds by keeping our minds open. Which brings us to our next rule.

FALL IN LOVE.

It might not be what you came for. It might not be practical. It might cost more than you want to spend. But if you're out antiquing and see something that you just can't get off your mind, in our experience, you should let yourself fall in love with it, and nab it right away.

Woodward Throwbacks' story, style, and mission have always been organic, developed over time by following our intuition. So if you're drawn to something unexpected, try to figure out why. By

making some impulse buys and learning how to fit them into your space, you'll develop your own one-of-a-kind sense of style, which is really what salvaging is all about.

Some rooms can be designed around one special object, like the hundred-year-old, 14-foot-long hardware display cabinet we repurposed into kitchen cabinets in the Loft House (page 47). But if you don't keep an open mind, these badass design moments may never happen. When you bring home something unusual that intrigues you, you're often bringing home inspiration as well.

DON'T SLEEP ON IT.

If you asked us about our biggest salvage regret, we'd tell you about an ornate wooden church pew Bo found on Facebook Marketplace, with individual seats separated by intricately carved armrests. But we asked ourselves—what could we do with a church pew? We slept on it. And the next morning, it was gone.

The FOMO ("fear of missing out," for any of you who don't use the internet) was so strong on this one that we even reached out to the Facebook Marketplace seller, to ask if they would connect us with whoever bought it, so we could make an offer. (Needless to say, the seller declined to share any information.) We posted a general call on Instagram for anyone who knew anything about a very special church pew. This find that got away taught us an important lesson: if you love it, don't let it go.

Of course, there are limits to this rule (see rule 4), but this decisiveness has really served us well at Woodward Throwbacks. Being able to jump on opportunities to buy something interesting, start a new project, or take a big next step has helped us stay aligned with and committed to our mission—making cool stuff with whatever we can find around us. You can always deal with the consequences later. (For the record, unexpected consequences are usually pretty rad.)

We found that when we were starting our own business, there wasn't a lot of room for doubt—we had way too much else on our minds. And we'd advise other artists, creatives, entrepreneurs, and those aspiring for a Throwbacks look to trust their own intuition just as much. Don't sleep on it! (Within reason; again, see rule 4.)

YOU CAN'T SALVAGE EVERYTHING.

This is where the voice of reason (Kyle) comes in. There is a fine line between salvaging and hoarding, and usually that fine line is made up of the thinnest little sliver of good judgment.

You may have fallen in love with something (rule 2). You may be imagining just how much you'll regret it if it's gone the next day (rule 3). But before you commit, ask yourself a few questions:

- *Will it fit in your car?* This is a simple but important consideration, unless you happen to have a friend with a pickup truck.
- *Can you store it?* You may not be able to jump on this project right away. And if you don't have a 24,000-square-foot warehouse, you might have to be okay with those massive oak beams sitting in your basement for weeks. (Or months. Or years.)
- *What's in your workshop?* Do you have the space, tools, and skills you'll need to make this diamond-in-the-rough find into the finished piece you're dreaming up? The equipment you have on hand might play a role in deciding whether to pull the trigger on a salvage job. If you don't have the right tools at the ready, see if you can borrow them from a friend or tool library nearby. And if you don't have the gadgets or the experience you need to fix something up, be prepared to find and pay the craftspeople who do.
- *What resources do you have at your disposal?* Not everybody has the hours or money to experiment with salvaged materials in the workshop (even we don't have as much time as we'd like to do that

these days). Depending on the time and labor you're willing to put in, it may make more sense to buy new materials or hire the right experts, and save all that effort for something else.

MAKE FRIENDS.

Community is important to us at Woodward Throwbacks, which should come as no surprise for a company that has relied on materials salvaged right in Detroit for most of its existence. We wouldn't have found half of the stuff we've geeked out about if we hadn't stayed curious, asked questions, and built and maintained connections throughout the city and beyond.

So start a conversation with your neighbor at a garage sale or when you see them taking on a new house project. Check out online communities, neighborhood organizations, and sites like Facebook Marketplace and Craigslist for special objects that need a new home. Even if you strike out, you'll be the first to come to mind when someone has some weird shit they want to off-load, and you'll probably come away with some stories that connect you more deeply to the people and places around you. You never know when a random conversation will lead to an epic find.

WELCOME TO DETROIT

YOU'LL FIND DETROIT IN EVERYTHING WE DO AT Woodward Throwbacks. Our story is written in the streets, bricks, and facades of this city. What we create is literally made of the wood, glass, and metal that built Detroit, and made in partnership with Detroiters, whether they were born here or drawn here like we were. This book shows you our Detroit, from objects full of history, to homes that preserve and push the city forward, to the creative, passionate people who live in them.

It's complicated but true that our business wouldn't be possible without the challenges Detroit has faced—systemic racism, disinvestment, corruption . . . just to name a few. But it's also true that our success is dependent on what makes this city great. Detroit isn't all dumpster diving for hidden gems—head downtown and you'll see that, bones to bones, we have some of the most beautiful architecture in the country.

In its heyday, Detroit was a place where architects and engineers from around the world came to build things, from the badass mosaic ceilings of the Guardian Building to the top-to-bottom marble of the Art Deco Fisher Building. Auto magnates and Motown execs lived in sprawling mansions made with only the best materials. Humbler but still special are the more modest single-family homes of the working-class people who built this city and still make it great, a reminder of a time when Detroit's booming economy allowed families to afford the American dream.

The contrasts in modern-day Detroit make you pay attention. Massive complexes like Fisher Body Plant 21—decaying, but still impressive—show off the city's former industrial chops. You'll pass a gorgeously maintained home with copper gutters, followed by a shabbier home with a beautifully tended garden, followed by a vacant lot. There's an honesty to Detroit that keeps you coming back, a gravitational pull in the contradictions, emptiness, and vibrant life.

But most of all, it's the people who make the city special. One of our favorite pieces of street art near Eastern Market reads "Detroit Never Left"—reminding anyone who thinks of Detroit as an urban wasteland that people always have been, are, and will be here. Talking to our neighbors or getting curious about someone doing renovations has led us to some of our best finds, favorite stories, and most loyal friendships. Detroiters have consistently invited us in and at the same time fiercely defended their city, inspiring us to preserve history while also making something new. They fill in the scars left by the hardships the city has gone through with art, action, celebrations, and community gardens, and many visitors find there's a space here for them as well.

So stop by if you haven't already—or give the city another chance if you haven't been in a while. You may just find that you want to move here, too.

INDUSTRIAL

WHEN WE CALL A SPACE "INDUSTRIAL," we're talking about a kind of rawness to the rooms and the materials that fill them. This could range from the entire building, like the former auto shop that has been adapted into the Forge House (page 33), to the objects within, like the old dumpster-dived sign that's now a central piece of art in the more traditional Victorian Home Base (page 59). Key for us with spaces and objects like these is taking the colder, harder, grittier feel of metal and bricks and concrete and incorporating them into a home environment, so these materials feel comfortable and even cozy. While all the houses in this section are homey, the authentic toughness and original patinas show through, expanding our definition of what a "home" can be.

THE FORGE HOUSE

The idea of some spaces is so romantic, they become archetypes. When you hear "artist loft" or "live/work space," you probably imagine exposed brick, high ceilings, and evidence of artmaking everywhere. This home in a converted industrial building is owned by an artist, and it fulfills many of those expectations—but without becoming cliché. It feels so original because it's filled with objects that are precious to the owner, and because it's been gradually renovated, bit by bit, by the artist himself.

The loft is actually two buildings. The records for the central structure, where the owner, Eric, lives, date back to 1906, and the shop where he works was built around the original building in 1960. For Eric, who's a metalworker, finding a space like this was the fulfillment of an aspiration that started when he was just a kid, when he says seeing graffiti in Detroit gave him permission to be an artist.

As an adult, he spent two years cruising around the city looking for buildings that might fit his dream of a live-in studio, going downtown to look at maps and writing letters to the owners of long-disused spaces. But even though he found the perfect space, it needed work. Over about a decade, he completed projects piecemeal as time and money allowed, and spent a not insignificant amount of time camping out in the building with just a woodstove for heat.

It all sounds a bit like an urban legend, but the result is a moody, personal, art-filled space that undeniably feels like a home. We've named this loft the Forge House because, yes, a metalworker lives here, but also because all the elements of this home combine to fire our imaginations.

FAVORITE MOMENTS

Can we say a space as a whole is a favorite moment? Because this loft is such a badass example of adaptive reuse, we can't help gushing about it.

Remember back in the introduction when we were talking a bit about what we do? The closest definition of it we've come across is adaptive reuse—the process of adapting an existing object, material, or space for a different purpose. And this loft is a perfect example: the owner has taken a formerly industrial space and made it into his house.

At first this concept might seem intimidating. It's not always easy to visualize how to create a home in a space that wasn't built for that purpose. And while the Forge House doesn't match up with the typical idea of "home," in some ways, it still feels cozy and authentic to the owner.

Plants and very personal art objects are scattered throughout the space. Beautiful mosaics, many made of salvaged tile from Detroit's famed Pewabic Pottery, add color and intimacy. This industrial space has a lot of metal details, but choosing some warmer gold and bronze tones for the bedframe and the light fixtures cozies up a material that's often thought of as cold and hard. Altogether this adapted industrial space feels honest and intimate rather than mechanical and intimidating.

We also love the metal bookshelf made by the artist and stuffed to the brim with his personal library. We're not huge fans of neat and tidy bookshelves, or ones organized by color, so we love this perfectly imperfect, helter-skelter collection. The way the books are tilted and piled on top of one another in no particular order shows that you don't need to be precious about how objects are arranged for them to look beautiful.

ABOVE: Eric's perfectly imperfect bookshelf, which he made himself, is one of our favorite moments in the Forge House.

OPPOSITE: The bathroom is filled with irreverent details, like colorful salvaged tiles from Pewabic Pottery, a famed Detroit ceramics studio.

SNAG THE STYLE

Even if you're not living in a former bump shop, the Forge House can teach you a lot about how to make any space into a home.

GO BIG

You can't talk about this loft without mentioning the cast-iron spiral staircase. Taking center stage, surrounded by filtered light and hanging plants, it also comes with a great story: Eric salvaged it (along with that collection of tiles from Pewabic Pottery, a famed Detroit ceramic studio founded in the beginning of the twentieth century) from a school that was being demolished in the city's Southwest neighborhood. He needed to disassemble it piece by piece in order to get it into his space; he also reworked the railings with brass and twisty pieces of salvaged metal, and painstakingly removed the purple paint it had once been covered in. But we

We're not necessarily suggesting that you put a motorcycle in your living room, but we want the Forge House to inspire you to be bold and not limit yourself to conventional ideas of home and the things you use to furnish and decorate it. If a room is offering you an opportunity for drama, the unexpected, or a major statement, we'd almost always tell you to go for it—especially if the big pieces in question also happen to be objects that bring you joy.

GET PERSONAL

Like the spiral staircase, almost every object in the loft has a personal story, whether it's a hand-me-down, gift, memento, or found object. A trio of bar-stools once belonged to Eric's grandfather; much of the art in the space was made by friends; the collar of a dearly departed dog hangs on a wall.

We like this way of thinking about decorating, like a personal museum of your own life. Though going out and looking for on-theme, color-coordinated art can be fun, it's way more Throwbacks Home to take stock of what you already have and curate the precious objects that, when put on display, can become works of art. Maybe you can bring your childhood action-figure collection into your stylish adulthood by arranging it on a shelf, or a hand-made card from a friend can find a place on your gallery wall. Stop automatically saying no to your relative who's downsizing and always trying to off-load their stuff on you. At least take a look—you might find something with a story attached that is a beautiful addition to your space.

think all that effort was totally worth it. This stunning staircase is a salvage job, a piece of art, an architectural feature, and a functional way to get from floor to floor, all in one.

For us, this is a key lesson to take away from the loft: don't shy away from creating your home on a dramatic, grand scale. Even in smaller and more traditional spaces, an unusual found object or an outsized piece of furniture can become a keystone if you figure out how to cleverly incorporate it into your house. Among other "go big" moments in the Forge House: huge works of art, many made by friends; Eric's motorcycle parked next to the kitchen, acting like a sculpture that recalls the building's automotive past; and actual sculptures created by the artist, looking perfectly at home despite their large scale and filling up space in the multistory, open parts of the loft.

ABOVE: Several of the owner's own works are on display throughout the Forge House.

OPPOSITE: The warm tone of the stately antique brass bedframe makes the lofted bed feel cozy.

Q + A WITH ERIC

Q: HOW DOES LIVING HERE SUIT YOUR LIFESTYLE?

A: At first it was just practical—it's that whole "if you want your tools there tomorrow, you better sleep there tonight" thing. It was also nice not having to pay rent in two different places over the years. But the loft is also a showcase for my work. If a potential client wants to get to know who I am, I can bring them here. Ideally, the clients I work with are people who like how I interpret the world. But even if someone doesn't exactly "get" me or the loft, I think there's a certain amount of respect for the space—like, "Okay, kid, I see what you're doing here."

Q: WHAT WENT INTO MAKING AN INDUSTRIAL SPACE THE HOME WE SEE TODAY?

A: It took about ten years to get the space to how you see it now, and I'd say three of those ten years were hard camping, with just the woodstove and a blanket. Times were tough, and there was no money in the city. It was a huge milestone when I got the floors done, which took another three to four years. There's something about waking up and walking barefoot to the kitchen to make coffee that makes you feel at home.

Really, though, making a home takes a lifetime, and even though it's a lot of work, I feel blessed to have the opportunity to improve this place—not everybody has the ability to do that. I'm very grateful.

Q: WHAT HAS SURPRISED YOU ABOUT THE PROCESS OF RENOVATING?

A: I'm genuinely surprised by how much I've enjoyed having a nice bathroom. In fact, I think I would have made it bigger if I'd known how much I'd like it.

Q: WHAT'S YOUR PROCESS FOR DECORATING YOUR SPACE?

A: It's kind of like that saying that the cobbler's kids have no shoes—I can make stuff for others, but the process of picking out stuff for me is torturous. At one point an ex-girlfriend set me straight—she was like, How many tables have I seen you make, and we're eating on a piece of plywood on top of a bucket? I credit her with snapping me out of it and me starting to get my shit together.

What ties everything together in this space is that it all has a story—they're heirlooms, things that have gotten handed down, the physical residual from important relationships. I really value using things that have already had a life.

OPPOSITE: A cast-iron spiral staircase, salvaged from a Detroit school that was slated for demolition.

METAL

In interior design, metal often takes a backseat to wood. Heavier and harder to work with, metal is often used as an accent rather than a primary material, but it can have a massive impact. Where wood is soft, organic, and textured, metal is usually sharp, rigid, and smooth, well suited to spaces with a more industrial vibe.

Still, metal is surprisingly versatile and comes in a wide range of colors—bronze to copper to steel—each with its own feel. Like wood, metal can be painted: we love the extra layers of color and detail paint adds to metal, especially when you find a chipped or rusted piece that's full of texture.

Not having the right tools is a barrier to entry when it comes to designing with metal, but metal is so much more adaptable than wood. Metal is flexible and can be bent into shapes that would be impossible for wood. Because metal can be skinny but still retain its strength, it adds unexpected lightness to a space where wood would feel bulky.

If you want to give a room a more modern, streamlined look, try to incorporate metal, even something as small as chrome cabinet hardware or a brass candlestick. Don't be afraid to look around and explore different kinds of metal and finishes—choosing a unique metal can totally transform your space.

ABOVE: A random selection of salvaged metals in the Woodward Throwbacks warehouse.

OPPOSITE: In the very industrial Forge House, a variety of metals mix: the golden glow of an Art Deco light fixture adds warmth, while the solid, steel, salvaged spiral staircase anchors the room.

Underneath the kitchen sink in the Raw and Refined house, we incorporated a piece of textured metal that was formerly part of the facade of an old diner.

More metal on metal in the Forge House: smooth chrome boomerang-shaped handles brighten utilitarian metal cabinets, making them more inviting to touch and open.

In the Garage House, the well-worn and chipped metal of the spiral staircase contrasts with the white walls and otherwise more polished space.

The brass faucet and handles in the Dreamy House's kitchen, handmade in Morocco, show just how warm and rustic metal can feel.

There's a mixture of metals here: cast-iron legs give our Ella dining table an industrial feel; a metal-and-glass room divider defines the space without blocking light; and brass light fixtures and cabinet hardware add a little class.

THE LOFT HOUSE

This nineteenth-century brick building is in Milwaukee Junction, a neighborhood named for its proximity to the intersection of several once-prominent railway systems. With such convenient access to train lines, this former industrial hub is full of beautiful brick warehouses, many of which are now being converted into that quintessential rustic and modern residence, the loft.

We were hired as designers to give this loft—composed of one long, wide-open room, with huge windows and lots of exposed brick—a facelift. It was a great opportunity to continue to prove one of our core concepts—that a sleek and beautiful product can be made mostly (or completely!) with salvaged materials. This renovation is also the story of a multiyear love affair with one amazing piece of furniture.

FAVORITE MOMENTS

The elephant in this room is without a doubt the massive, deep-red cabinet unit in the kitchen, accented with beautiful brass hardware. This piece would be stunning even if it didn't have a history, but it happens to have a great salvaging backstory.

This unit came from Detroit Hardware, a historic, woman-owned hardware store that was just short of one hundred years old when it sadly closed in 2018. When we heard the store was closing, we decided to stop by—and were floored to see all of the original hardware display units were still there and intact.

It took awhile for the owners to warm up to us. We spent some time helping to clean the place up, sweeping, taking out the trash. We wanted them to know we genuinely cared about their story and the history of their space. Being able to cultivate that sense of community only made the unit we were able to salvage feel that much more special.

The cabinet sat in our garage for about three years while we waited for the perfect opportunity to use such a unique and powerful piece; we didn't want to settle. When we saw this massive open space, we knew that the unit's time had finally come. The kicker? Detroit Hardware used to be just down the street from the building where the cabinets now live. It felt like we were bringing the piece back home.

We put in a ton of work to make sure that the cabinets not only looked beautiful but also were a functional part of a modern kitchen. We extended the unit to integrate a sink and a fridge, and built all new trim profiles from scratch to perfectly blend everything in. The stone countertops were salvaged from Detroit's Marygrove College, which shut its doors in 2019. The result looks like a custom, high-end built-in—but not many kitchens can boast a 14-foot-long, hundred-year-old hardware display cabinet with a history deeply rooted in their city.

The other thing that makes this space is the metal-and-glass room divider. Roominess is part of a loft's appeal, but a long, open-concept room—just floors and brick walls—can present a design challenge. Creating some separation between the kitchen and the living/entertainment/dining room was key, and this room divider is our best-case scenario. The custom-fabricated metal room divider is substantial and industrial, but the huge, wide opening and airy glass keep things feeling spacious and ensure that one area isn't totally cut off from the other.

SNAG THE STYLE

We learned a lot while designing this space that we're excited to share with you.

TRUST YOUR GUT

Nothing makes you question your vision for a space more than an endless stream of design decisions. The biggest question we ran into in the Loft House was what color to paint the all-important hardware display cabinet that became the backbone of the kitchen.

Bo wanted to use red paint for this piece; she was inspired by all the brick hues throughout the room and thought a rich, deep red and brass hardware would be the perfect, refined complement. But red is a tricky shade, one she hadn't worked with much before. She visited all the paint shops around town and hadn't found anything quite right. She started to rethink everything: if she couldn't find the right red, then maybe she was wrong about the color—and if she wasn't right about that, what else might she be overlooking? But then she stopped by Mostek, our friendly neighborhood automotive paint and glass shop, just across from our Hamtramck warehouse. She saw the deep, almost maroon red that she ultimately used for the hardware cabinet while flipping through a color swatch booklet, and the

Mostek guys trusted her to take the booklet to a paint store for a color match.

We're really glad we stuck with Bo's original vision for the space, even if it took a little extra effort to make it a reality. We hope this story gives you the confidence to follow through on your crazy idea too. If you put in the work to bring your off-the-wall design to fruition, the result is often something you'll never see anywhere else—and that's beautiful.

FIND YOUR KEYSTONE

There are a lot of textures and styles in the Loft House. Colors range from the deep red of the kitchen cabinets, to the warm salvaged wood of the island and dining table, to the black minibar. A few different metals are used—brass for the cabinet hardware and pendant lights, black for the room divider and other light fixtures. And the furniture and objects throughout—all salvage—range from rustic to industrial to modern. What holds it all together? Using the same salvaged marble for both the kitchen countertops and the top of the bar in the living/dining area.

ABOVE: A custom-made room divider, constructed of metal and glass, makes this huge, open space feel less overwhelming.

The metal-and-glass room divider separates the loft into two distinct spaces: the kitchen and the dining/entertainment area. But using the same stone in both areas ensures they still talk to each other. In big, open-concept spaces like this, it's important to create some separation between different areas, while also making sure everything's in harmony.

BUILT-INS AS A BASE

The huge, open-concept nature of many lofts presents a design challenge: it can be hard just to decide what goes where. The owner of the Loft House didn't even mind if we moved the (once very tiny) kitchen, the only feature that was really anchoring the space. For a designer or decorator, this flexibility can be freeing, or the number of options for laying out the room can paralyze you.

Built-ins were our main solution for making this cavernous space feel natural and decisive. The beauty and massive scale of the kitchen cabinet unit, bespoke island, metal-and-glass room divider, and long dry bar and storage bench (all constructed of reclaimed materials) make this space feel finished and easy to understand. Even some of the smaller pieces of furniture have a built-in element: a few awesome chairs salvaged from the Thirty-Sixth District Court are bolted to the ground.

Incorporating built-ins into your space may take a little more foresight and effort, but the custom feel they bring to your home is a gift that keeps on giving. These unique, thoughtful pieces of furniture, objects with a story that will last for generations, have a sense of permanence, unlike the cheap, disposable feel of today's mass-produced furniture. So be on the lookout for opportunities to add some built-ins to your house, from a bespoke bookshelf to a wardrobe worthy of your favorite clothes. We promise the extra work will be worth it.

ABOVE: The bolted-down swivel chair feels both playful and permanent in the Loft House, a world away from the courtroom it was salvaged from.

Q + A WITH BO + KYLE

Q: WHAT IS CHALLENGING ABOUT DESIGNING A LOFT SPACE?

A: Being able to revamp an example of the quintessentially urban space that is a converted loft is the stuff of Detroit designer dreams, but this project came with two main difficulties. First, we needed to create some separation between spaces like the kitchen and the living areas. Second, we challenged ourselves to build in salvaged materials in a modern and clean way that wasn't too in-your-face.

The challenge of these huge, open spaces that are kind of a blank slate is not just delineating between different areas in the room but also making the whole thing feel cozy. Picking out furniture that's the right scale to fill up the space is important, and so is choosing the right accessories. When you zoom in on the details, you want them to feel homey and personal; that's a big part of making a large loft space feel like home.

Q: IT SOUNDS LIKE THE HARDWARE CABINET WAS A GREAT ANCHOR PIECE TO BUILD THIS LOFT AROUND— HOW DID YOU THINK ABOUT THE OTHER FURNITURE AND BUILT-INS IN THIS SPACE?

A: We designed more massive built-ins that could hold their own with the hardware cabinet—and all of them were created from salvaged materials as well. On the other side of the glass-and-metal room divider, we built a huge, 20-foot-long piece that's a mixture of a credenza, bar cabinet, and bench, made from reclaimed oak. The kitchen island is made from salvaged church pews, and the marble on both was claimed from Marygrove College in Detroit, which closed in 2019.

We wanted even the more portable pieces of furniture to have a substantial feel. The dining table is from our Ella Collection, made of solid, rich, raw wood and heavy metal legs that have an industrial feel.

Q: WHAT'S DIFFERENT ABOUT THE PROCESS OF DESIGNING FOR A CLIENT VERSUS DESIGNING FOR YOURSELF?

A: When it's your own space, you have a bit more freedom to make off-the-wall choices, because you know what you like. In the case of the cabinets we ended up using in this loft, for example, we'd had them for a long time before we ultimately installed them here. Over the years, we had a few different ideas for how to use them in one of our own spaces that didn't pan out. When we were thinking about incorporating the cabinets into spaces that we were designing for ourselves, we were planning to keep the original crackly, minty green paint and add in a bright orange, very retro fridge. It was a pretty wild design. But at the end of the day, when you're designing for a client, you know someone else has to live in the space you're creating and love it. So the design we came up with here was much more simplified and elegant.

Q: WHAT DO YOU THINK THIS SPACE SAYS ABOUT YOU AS DESIGNERS?

A: We always love an opportunity to seamlessly integrate huge salvaged pieces like the hardware display unit into a space. It was exciting to put a salvage twist on something as essential and everyday as kitchen cabinets, and the millwork and other built-ins here, from the kitchen island to the bar/credenza/bench, are equally special (and all salvage, too).

Hopefully, everyone who walks into the loft will give some thought to the objects here and where they came from. But even though the materials have history, the furniture is still sleek and modern. You might have to tell someone that some of these pieces are salvage, and that subtle use of reused materials is something we're always trying to achieve. The coffee table, from our Leftovers Collection, epitomizes that—all of the pieces of mahogany that make up the surface were reclaimed from an old boatyard on the Detroit River. But assembled together like a mosaic under an epoxy, the table looks totally polished. This space is proof that salvage doesn't have to be rustic, and that's kind of our thing.

HUTCHES AND CABINETS

Maybe more than any other pieces of furniture, hutches and cabinets can make or break a space. The owners of the homes featured in this book told us again and again that they loved these beautiful yet functional storage solutions—particularly their hutches—more than anything else in their house.

Until you see how beautiful these pieces can be, and the variety they can offer, it's easy to think of them as more utilitarian than anything. They're places for hiding away your ugly stuff, not beautiful objects in themselves, right? But when you give them more thought, you realize hutches and cabinets should be statement pieces in their own right. They often have open shelves or glass doors, which tells you they're places to put your favorite items on display as well as put away the things that aren't as pretty. And what other piece of furniture takes up as much vertical space and makes the same impact in a room?

Hutches and cabinets can be expensive, and when you're stuck with cheaper ones, you often want to hide them away. But there are tons of creative options for storing your stuff that are supposed to stand out, and they don't have to cost a fortune. You can find an awesome vintage hutch for a great price, especially if you're willing to put some elbow grease into restoring it with a fresh coat of paint. Salvaged upper and lower cabinets can be found way cheaper than custom ones and will still give you an upscale look. And unique hardware alone can go a long way to fancying up your storage solutions—whether you make your own funky ceramic knobs like the ones in the Mosaic House (page 213), or find some special pulls with a story in an antique store.

Put it all together, and hutches and cabinets are pieces that are meant to be cherished, that make a house feel like a home.

ABOVE: In some cases, antique hutches are almost like folk art: this hundred-plus-year-old piece was probably created from whatever the person who made it had on hand.

OPPOSITE: An antique hutch is a favorite piece and place to display cherished items in the Dreamy House.

Okay, so this isn't exactly a hutch. But we love the use of salvaged school lockers for storage in the Garage House for the story and pop of color they provide.

A special hutch in the Charming House that once lived in the offices of the *Detroit Free Press*.

The kitchen storage in the Loft House is not only beautiful, it also has a story: it was originally a display cabinet from a historic hardware store that used to be no more than a few blocks away.

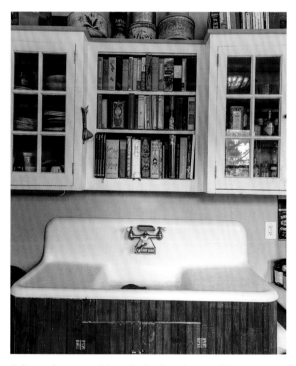

Salvaged upper cabinets in the Renaissance House kitchen look like they were always meant to be there.

Handmade ceramic handles add character to the original cabinets in the Mosaic House.

THE HOME BASE

Welcome to the prototypical Throwbacks Home—our very own place in Corktown, a 1901 Victorian that Bo bought in 2014. The neighborhood around the house has changed a ton over the years; even before Ford came in to turn the historic train station down Michigan Avenue into its new tech hub, developers and condos and hotels and restaurants were arriving in droves. But the house itself has changed a lot since we moved in, too.

When Bo bought it, the house looked like it hadn't been touched since a very 1970s remodel—and it had been occupied by heavy smokers since then. There was wallpaper and wall-to-wall carpeting; we ripped it out within two hours of closing, and had some adventures in floor refinishing and wall cleaning (FYI, LA's Totally Awesome cleaner is really pretty awesome). Woodward Throwbacks was just getting started, so for a while the sunroom was our sanding room, the garage was our woodshop, and we did our packaging in the living room and screen-printing in the basement. One of the reasons we ultimately decided to get a separate shop and storefront was so we could get some distance from the business and make the house feel like a home.

But even after our business outgrew this house, it's served not only as our home base but also as a touchstone for how Woodward Throwbacks has evolved over the years, a testing ground for a lot of our products, furniture, and concepts. It was

here that Bo chose to paint the window trim black on a whim (Kyle wasn't amused), and where we decided to switch out the janky subway-tile backsplash in our kitchen with salvaged slate chalkboards the night before the photo shoot for this book (true story).

It might surprise you to learn that even though we work in the furniture and interior design business, our house is not perfect—far from it. Though it might look aspirational from afar or on Instagram, the irony is that with all the things we always have going on, our own home often gets the short shrift. This home is a decade-plus work in progress, and we're very much okay with that.

Decorated in the quintessential Throwbacks Home mix of styles and eras, the Home Base is hard to characterize, but a commercial-grade range in the kitchen and gritty adaptive reuse art and objects ultimately led us to put our house in the "industrial" category. But as usual, the labels don't matter too much to us. What has always been important to us is that this space feels cozy, warm, and like it belongs to us. Every time we make a change, or bring in a new piece of art or furniture, we're contemplating, over and over again, what home means to us.

FAVORITE MOMENTS

What really sold Bo on this place when she was walking through it was the massive, industrial-grade range, a statement piece in the otherwise pretty ordinary kitchen. Legend has it that the previous owner, who also owned the now-closed Casey's Pub across the street (RIP), would cook food for the bar here when it got busy.

This view of the kitchen is still one of our favorite moments in the house. The stove is an eye-catching example of adaptive reuse (a commercial range being used in a residential kitchen), accented by cabinets that we painted black for extra drama, butcher-block counters, and a salvaged lath ceiling. The most recent (we're talking down to the wire) addition? A backsplash made of reclaimed chalkboards.

So, yes, we only installed the slate backsplash the night before the photo shoot for this book (during which we got about three hours of sleep put together). It was a project we'd been thinking about for a while—we had all these beautiful salvaged chalkboards, hated the subway-tile backsplash we'd sloppily installed sometime before,

ABOVE: The powder room (finally) received an update as a pandemic project. We're obsessed with the green glazed pedestal sink (a salvage find) and the paint color, Golden Mist by Benjamin Moore.

OPPOSITE: Sweet Ginger the Shopdog lounging on a couch in the living room, one of our favorite spaces in the Home Base.

and loved the idea of creating a backsplash out of large solid pieces of material rather than individual pieces of tile. Sure, we didn't get around to it until the last minute, but we love how it turned out. The green slate doesn't automatically read "chalkboard," though you could in theory write all over it with chalk if you wanted to—and it's conveniently easy to clean with soap and water. It's another material in our kitchen with a story, and introduces another color to the space.

It's tough to pick just one other favorite moment in the house, but if pressed we would have to say the living room. When we found the awesome Victorian couch on Craigslist and nestled it into this space, we truly fell in love with it, and the rest of the furniture and art fell into place from there. We're not usually huge fans of velvet, but the material just works here—especially in contrast with the more industrial objects in the space, and when the light hits the room just right. The couch is

Pictured here, a few views of our dining room: favorite objects displayed on open shelves, a mirrored piece of art, and of course, one of our Ella tables.

framed by some of our favorite pieces of art in the house—an ad featuring a glamorous Black couple skiing, and some nineteenth-century oval portraits with curved glass—and paired with a vintage mid-century side table and one of our coffee tables made from repurposed wood flooring. Altogether, it's the perfect napping spot, a cozy mix of eras and styles and materials that just plain makes us happy to look at.

SNAG THE STYLE

The Home Base is our laboratory, so we probably have more lessons to share from this space than from anywhere else.

KEEP IT LIGHT

Since we make furniture and design spaces for a living, our own home often gets the short shrift. But when something finally does get done in our house, it usually happens in a sudden burst of energy—and we have a ton of fun in the process.

Sometimes we finally get around to a project because we're coming up against a deadline (like the slate backsplash in our kitchen, installed just before a photo shoot). Sometimes we've just been staring at a room we hate for too long, and randomly start ripping out fixtures and picking out new paint colors. That's what happened with our first-floor powder room, which Bo remodeled over several weekends in 2021. (Hot tip: if you're taking on house projects you've never done before, like plumbing and electricity, it can be a good idea to start with the smallest room possible.)

In the case of our sunroom makeover, we found ourselves with a ton of unexpected time on our hands. When the world shut down because of Covid, our business was paused, the future was uncertain, and we needed a place to hang outside, so we took the opportunity to finally upgrade this indoor/outdoor space (which had formerly been a plant graveyard). To make it more fun, we challenged ourselves to do it without buying anything new for the space—finding ways to use salvaged stuff we'd been keeping in the garage, shopping our home, and even driving around looking for the perfect branch to serve as the base for the hanging light fixture.

The moral of the story is that even as design professionals, we don't force it. We try to seize the energy and time when they come, and to make every project as enjoyable as possible. Put some music on, crack a beer, experiment with a material you've never used before. If you aren't having fun, what's the point?

WHY SO SERIOUS?

We put so much pressure on ourselves when it comes to our homes. We hear from people all the time who are upset and embarrassed that it's taking so long for their house to feel "finished."

We and our work-in-progress home are here to offer some perspective. We do this stuff professionally, and most of our upstairs rooms are still a disaster. Some of our rooms just sing, like the living room and the sunroom (especially when that perfect light hits). But other areas need work, and we've also embarked on projects that turned out to be not such a good idea in retrospect.

The big lesson we want people to take away from this house is that that's okay! Our homebase is an ongoing project, and we know it will keep evolving over the years. We're always changing, redoing, and moving things around, and we like to think of that as a trial-and-error process of falling in love with our space, again and again. Permission granted to make mistakes, keep it light, and take time to enjoy your life both in and outside your home, even if you bought a somewhat chaotic fixer-upper that never quite feels finished. A true salvage-and-design nerd knows that a house is always a work in progress.

OPPOSITE: It's fun to play with different shades of green in the plants and glassware next to our salvaged slate chalkboard backsplash.

THROWBACKS HOME INTERIORS

One of our favorite views in the house. We made the credenza using wood salvaged from church pews and an incredible old sign we found in upstate New York. The wonderfully weird old sign on the wall above it advertises a long-defunct Detroit bar.

WUBZEES BRAND

BAR & GRILL

Steamed HOT DOGS

RALPH

HAMBURGS · GRI

Q + A WITH BO + KYLE

Q: DO YOU HAVE A FAVORITE PIECE THAT YOU MADE IN YOUR HOME?

A: We love the bar cabinet made from an old sign in our living room. We have a few other Woodward Throwbacks pieces in the house, like our dining and coffee tables, but for whatever reason that piece just feels like a statement of purpose for us, of where we're going as designers. It looks like it was meant to be there, underneath another old sign that's one of our favorite pieces of art, and its color complements the rest of the room so perfectly.

Q: HOW DO YOU GO ABOUT BUILDING YOUR PERSONAL ART COLLECTION?

A: There are two specific kinds of art we're working on collecting: one is found and salvaged old signs, and the other is art by Black artists or with Black subjects. We love the Larry Heyer's ad featuring two Black skiers that's hanging in the living room for that reason; it's from the 1920s, and it's just so rare to see images of Black people that are so elegant and posh from that era. A favorite in the old-signs category is the metallic, slightly iridescent Road Closed sign over the opening into the kitchen; that was dumpster-dived, has awesome texture, and fits perfectly in the long, narrow area where it's hung.

In most cases, we gravitate toward a piece of art when we've never seen anything like it before. Like the Wubzee's Bar & Grill sign over our bar cabinet. This thing is so fucking weird. It's a beautifully hand-painted sign, but it's also a piece of plywood,

and the logo is bizarre: a dog with a mustache wearing a helicopter hat and sunglasses, smoking a cigar, in front of the Detroit skyline. There's nothing else like it, and there are lots of examples of one-of-a-kind pieces like that in our house. We like art that makes you look twice, references obscure bits of history, and asks questions that can't really be answered. Decorating with pieces like these is like filling your house with Easter eggs.

It's so fun to continue to develop our interests as art collectors, and to focus in on specific kinds of pieces when we're out shopping. Limiting our finds to specific mediums, subjects, or artists makes a collection feel cohesive rather than random—even if everything's still somewhat eclectic.

Q: WHERE ARE YOUR FAVORITE PLACES TO HANG OUT IN THE HOUSE?

A: You'll often find Bo hanging in the kitchen, and Kyle napping on our favorite yellow couch, but in the summer, we're usually in the sunroom. It's the best spot for coffee in the morning or cocktails at night. We updated this space as a Covid project and didn't buy anything new for it—everything was found, reclaimed, or just shopped from our own house. This adds extra texture to everything there and makes it even more special. With the vines growing in from the alley next door over the screen windows, there's so much privacy, but you still get to be outside. Hanging out there feels like you're hanging in a tree. It's fabulous.

Q: WHAT'S YOUR NEXT BIG HOUSE PROJECT?

A: Let's be honest: for every perfectly curated room in these pictures, there's another room in our house that is definitely not photo shoot ready. At this point that's the whole upstairs and our TV room, and we'll probably need to redo our hundred-year-old floors at some point. But that's okay! We know that it will all get done eventually and will look great. In the meantime, we always have a ton of other stuff to focus on.

That said, the next big thing we're thinking about is adding more color to the house. We used to be a little reluctant to use bright color—the walls in our house are mostly white or dark, like the green in the dining room. But we love the bright orange we used in our powder room makeover, and it's inspired us to try to incorporate more color into other rooms.

OLD SIGNS

Decorating and designing with old signs is one of our signatures, and we hope all the readers of this book will start thinking about these pieces as works of art. Here's why.

Old signs have been a huge part of our brand since the beginning. That's partially because we have a wealth of beautiful old signs at our fingertips—hand-painted signs are a Detroit specialty. The ability to make them is a dying art form, and when we say art form, we mean it—just like a great painting, you can see the brushstrokes on these old signs and imagine the hand that made them. They're personal and intimate, and inevitably start a conversation. They may have spelling errors or use unexpected language or imagery. They make you ask questions about who made them and where they come from.

Sure, these pieces might not work for every space. But they're more versatile than you might think, and if you look around, you'll see awesome examples of old signs throughout thrift shops and antique stores. Depending on a sign's design, color palette, and the room that it's placed in, it can fit in a space that's industrial and gritty, or modern and more refined. Like we said, we want people to start thinking of old signs as fine art—because that's what they are.

ABOVE: The colors of this cabinet, part of our Hardware Store Sign Collection, go perfectly with the Cosmopolitan House's moody palette.

OPPOSITE: In the Old Meets New House, a beautiful old sign not only looks great but also makes you ask questions: What car? What world record? Where?

The gritty texture of an old sign can also look modern and refined in the right setting—like this example in the bright and airy Dreamy House.

A perfectly imperfect beauty salon sign holds its own next to fine art in the Gallery House.

Two signs in conversation at the Home Base—one hung on the wall as art, the other turned into a statement piece of a credenza.

This sign, an old menu from a restaurant in L.A., adds texture and interest to an otherwise minimal bedroom.

THE GARAGE HOUSE

In Core City, just two miles northwest of downtown, there are more empty lots than occupied homes, but there's a spirit of experimentation, of rethinking the way living in a city could be. Futuristic Quonset huts sit next to urban farms, and there's a commitment to development that doesn't squeeze as much profit as possible out of a block. This house takes the same innovative, think-outside-the-box approach to making a home.

This house is a new build, the only nonhistorical home in the book. But far from having a cookie-cutter vibe, this recently constructed house uses salvage materials and vintage objects in a way that feels extremely personal and perfectly suited to the owner's preferences and lifestyle. It's bright, airy, and modern, but its curved wall and industrial materials were inspired by an automotive garage, and we love the way the space plays with the contrast between sleek and textured, Detroit's history as well as its future.

The goal of the owner, François, was to create an open, multiuse house, and you can see lots of inspirations behind the design besides the garage it's named for, from an art gallery to a skate park to a movie theater. None of those spaces are necessarily reminiscent of home, but somehow, the Garage House is still totally homey.

FAVORITE MOMENTS

This spiral staircase is a salvage find—and it's a good one. Instead of refinishing it with polished, brand-new paint, the owner left the texture, patina, cracks, and rust untouched, offering the best contrast with the rest of the bright, white, modern, open-concept room that takes up the entire first floor. It took a lot of effort to get the staircase here: found using Facebook Marketplace, it was located in Chicago and originally built for a three-story space, so it had to be deconstructed, moved, and adjusted to suit the two-story Garage House before it could be installed.

A spiral is always a huge, dramatic moment. But despite all the work needed to make it fit, the choice of a salvaged spiral staircase is actually as practical as it is cool and aesthetically pleasing. This historic staircase is made of steel, while newer aluminum versions François saw seemed less sturdy.

Our other favorite moment is the huge curved wall of windows next to the front door, which light up the entire first floor when the sun is shining. We want to highlight this architectural, structural element because we think it really makes the whole place. This massive source of natural light is the perfect companion for a variety of very healthy plants, and it sets the space up to be an ideal art gallery for the work of artist Karana Devidasi, highlighting all the large-scale paintings decorating the walls. In a nice design moment, the unique curve of the wall also echoes the spiral of the staircase in the center of the room, in addition to reflecting the curved walls of the auto garages that inspired this house.

Maybe more than any other home in this book, the Garage House is filled with light and expansive space, and the rounded wall of windows is a big part of that, setting up the main room to feel airy and bright, serving as a contrast to heavier elements like the concrete floor and spiral staircase. When it comes to filling a house with objects you love versus giving them room to breathe, it's always a delicate balance, and we think the Garage House walks the line perfectly.

OPPOSITE: The light-filled space of the Garage House is the perfect place for houseplants and playful objects like a Lucite table, which amplifies all the sunlight.

SNAG THE STYLE

This space is full of unexpected, imaginative, and inspiring objects and design decisions.

UNUSUAL OBJECTS

A lot of the furniture in the Garage House deserves an extra look, because it's made of unusual objects and materials. One of our favorite examples: the gas canisters that have been repurposed as barstools for the kitchen island. It was François's

The Garage House is characterized by bright white walls, an abundance of natural light, and playful pops of color.

idea to put cushions on these beautiful industrial objects and turn them into seating. (Hot tip: they also make great planters.)

Then there are the vintage lockers being used for storage, with atmosphere and patina galore. François was fascinated by the lockers as an object, because he says that lockers aren't really used in schools in France, where he's from. Even the coffee table is unusual: made of Lucite that interacts with all the light from the huge windows, it shows off the industrial concrete floor below.

In each of these cases, the novelty of using something unorthodox as an everyday object draws you in—they offer a great visual that just plain has more interest than objects being used for exactly the purpose they were made for. But they're also practical: the gas canister barstools are lightweight and comfortable, and the lockers have plenty of room to tuck away clutter. Thinking outside the box about the furniture in your space, and the materials that they are made of, is one of our very favorite things to do as designers. We think this is even more essential in a new build. Older, more unusual objects add character and warmth that make this space feel lived-in instead of sterile and bland.

GET OUT OF THE HOUSE

In addition to making his home livable, François wanted it to be a place where artist friends could display their work and filmmakers could premiere their movies, reflecting his very social and thoughtful lifestyle. Hence the gallery vibes, with all the great light and massive white walls for displaying art, and the projector screen that stylishly descends in front of the curved glass windows. It's clear that François's house was primarily inspired by an automotive garage, but also that he was equally interested in a home that could double as an art museum, or a salon. In a reference to movies and the theater, a huge, almost sculptural spotlight hangs out by a metal shelf of happy-looking plants. This statement piece is also functional, providing a

source of light (at night, François uses it to light up his disco ball).

If you ever get stuck when it comes to creating a house that suits your lifestyle, try thinking of other spaces that inspire you and foster your hobbies. Maybe you're a cyclist and want to check out your local bike shop to learn how to store your bikes in a way that's both beautiful and functional. Maybe you're an artist and need to think about which room in your house has the most light, potential for storage, ability to absorb a mess, and space to move around, before deciding what goes where. Taking an intuitive approach to design that reflects how you actually spend your time and leaves conventional ideas of the home behind can be really inspiring, and often results in a house that's totally unique.

Q + A WITH FRANÇOIS

Q: WHY DID YOU WANT TO BUILD A SPACE INSPIRED BY A GARAGE?

A: I originally had my eye on an actual garage in the historic Woodbridge neighborhood, not far from Midtown and closer to downtown, but it came on the market way more expensive than it should have been. I just loved the idea of adapting a space like that to my own home life and couldn't get it out of my head, so I decided to try to create that effect by custom-building my own house.

Q: HOW WOULD YOU DESCRIBE YOUR STYLE?

A: Honestly, I don't really have the vocabulary to describe it. Since I was building the space, I had a blank canvas to work with, so I started by thinking about other places that inspired me—like the automotive garage, of course, but also art galleries and skate parks and music venues. So the inspiration came more from thinking about the house and how I would live in it. It was important to me that the space was multiuse and could be adapted to any situation. I wanted it to be open and inviting and welcoming—like the living room, which is cozy but also opens up to the outside. The art and furniture in it is all just stuff that I like—I don't really put labels on it beyond that. It all just kind of fell into place.

Q: HOW DO YOU GO ABOUT FINDING FURNITURE AND ART AND PLACING IT IN YOUR SPACE?

A: I look everywhere from Facebook Marketplace to antique stores. I've had a lot of the objects here forever—like ten years or more. I've just been waiting for the right place to put them, moving them from apartment to apartment. In previous homes, big things like the vintage spotlight didn't quite fit, but here I have all the space that I could want. It's amazing to have an idea in your head of your space and how things might look in it for such a long time, and then to finally be able to make it a reality.

In terms of art, my girlfriend, Karana Devidasi, is an artist, and she made most of the paintings here. Especially in a very blank, white space like this, it's really important to me that the art provides those pops of color.

Q: WHAT MAKES THIS HOUSE FEEL LIKE HOME TO YOU?

A: I'm really still adapting to this space. It was designed to welcome a lot of people, and then Covid hit, which put a hold on big parties and events. When friends could come over, it all felt more real, and I could see that the house worked in the way I'd imagined. I still dream of hosting art shows and movie premieres here.

A favorite object in the Garage House: an antique spotlight.

LIGHT AND PLANTS

Let's talk about light. Great natural light is obviously a huge asset—an architectural holy grail. Since most of the homes in this book are historic, they tend to have awesome light; when they were built, artificial lighting wasn't great, so they had to make use of the sun as much as possible.

In a space that gets a lot of sunlight, we like to downplay artificial lighting and go with the rhythm of the day. This allows for dramatic moments as the sun travels through a room, and you can enhance the sunlight even more by placing transom windows, unique materials, or reflective objects in just the right spots.

But when it comes to how much light you have in your house, you only have so much control. Maybe you don't have tons of windows, or your home faces north, or is surrounded by leafy trees. No sweat: there are still plenty of opportunities to play with light. You can brighten things up with lighter paint or materials, or embrace the darkness in your colors and objects.

And in our experience, wherever there's light—even just a little of it—there are plants. Pretty much all the houses in this book have some greenery. (Yes, we're millennials and we love houseplants.) These are also objects that interact with light, growing toward it and happily soaking it up when the sun's shining. We love the extra texture and unpredictable, organic element they supply.

At the end of the day, whether you give in to the moodiness of a darker space or play up your natural light, great light is just plain sexy.

ABOVE: The natural light in the Dreamy House is a huge part of what makes it so, well, dreamy.

OPPOSITE: In the luminous Garage House, unique materials like the Lucite coffee table and chrome-and-leather lounge chairs interact with light in eye-catching ways.

A dramatic light moment in the Home Base's moody powder room—strong sunlight really plays up the contrast between the dark beadboard and orangey-yellow wall.

We'll never fully cut back the greenery covering the screened walls of our sunroom in the Home Base; they add privacy and the dreamiest filtered light.

Plants, draping down and growing up, add vertical interest to this view of the Mosaic House kitchen.

The Forge House has less natural light, which makes it even more dramatic as it changes throughout the day.

The transom window in the Old Meets New House doing its thing when the light hits.

MODERN

THINK "MODERN" AND YOU MAY SEE a light-filled space almost
devoid of textures, distracting colors, and unnecessary stuff—which
doesn't sound very Throwbacks Home on the surface. But a modern
home that really excites us incorporates texture and vintage thought-
fully, bringing a little something extra while still keeping it clean. We
love the challenge of creating a simple, smooth design that's easy on
the eyes, but full of detail and texture when you look more closely. A
modern Throwbacks Home doesn't have to be minimal.

THIS CAR WILL
ATTEMPT TO
Break
WORLD RECORD
going for
200 FEET

THE OLD MEETS NEW HOUSE

And now for our biggest project yet: an abandoned, fire-damaged brick home we purchased as a fixer-upper in 2020. We'd applied our foundational concept of making salvage materials sleek and modern to furniture and smaller interior design projects, but this was an entirely new challenge. You have to be slightly unhinged to see the potential in a place like this, but if you know us at all by now, it won't surprise you to hear we were truly stoked.

We're calling this space the Old Meets New House because despite the fact that it looks so sleek and modern, much if not most of the stuff in it is actually pretty old. The list of places we sourced materials from for this house reads like a map of the Detroit metro area: repurposed science lab tables from Marygrove College, stone from the beautiful downtown Book Tower skyscraper, and a mantel from a Corktown townhouse for starters. But the finished house doesn't scream salvage, and that's what we were going for. A simple, selective color palette really spotlights how crisp, clean, and polished these reclaimed materials can be. This space is still full of texture and personality, but there's room for the house's future owners to put their own personality into each room.

A lot of change has happened here. We turned a burned-out shell of a house into a clean, bright, quintessentially Throwbacks Home space. Looking at how far we've come, it's hard not to feel inspired by the power of using salvaged materials to transform a home; we hope you feel inspired, too.

FAVORITE MOMENTS

The kitchen is the true star of this house. Since we tore the place down to the studs, we had a virtual blank slate to work with; it was a chance for us to imagine our ideal kitchen, play with awesome built-ins, and figure out clever workarounds for some of the common inconveniences and eyesores that can plague this all-important room.

There are so many things we love in this space. We used paint-splattered old scaffolding for the shelves above the countertop, and the banquette and island are made of salvaged oak timbers, formerly church pews. The top of the dining table is made of the same material, but the legs are even cooler: they're actually old support columns that we found in the basement, and we love all the chipped, rusted texture. Even with the new stuff, we tried to take inspiration from what was already in the house. The color of the cabinets, for example, borrows from the tile flooring in the entryway, which was one of the house's only intact original details.

The boldest design decision is without a doubt the wall cladding. We loved the idea of bringing the retro, kind of seventies look that is wall paneling into the twenty-first century. We found a company that does timber-framed homes and milled down their scraps and split beams to create this awesome, very Up North, cabiny effect, and we loved using a reclaimed material to integrate the paneled fridge and tons of built-in storage. Because this wall is visible when you open the front door, it becomes a focal point for the whole house, and when the light comes through the glowy antique transom window above the back door, the kitchen is especially dreamy.

Our other favorite moment is the spiral staircase to the attic. A spiral always adds drama (that's probably why there are three in this book—we can't get enough of them), and it's also a great way to travel from floor to floor without needing to make huge changes to the roof above. We searched for the perfect staircase for a long time before turning to Instagram to see if anyone in our community had a lead, and got lucky: the spiral we ultimately found came from a house in Boston-Edison, just next door to the North End.

We used deep-green enamel paint, usually reserved for automotive work, to give the staircase a polished, glossy finish, and made use of what would otherwise be dead space behind the spiral to create a custom-made bench—the perfect, secret, "don't bother me" reading nook. Or a spot for all your plants. Whatever you prefer.

SNAG THE STYLE

There's no way you can come away from taking a house from about-to-collapse to move-in-ready without learning a few things.

CHECK THE BASEMENT

The first thing you should do whenever you buy a house or condo is check the basement and the closets. You might be lucky enough to find "new old stock" (containers of tile or wood or paint or other materials left over from earlier renovations)—old to the former owners, new to you. Or you might

discover cool objects to integrate into your space, like the structural columns we used as legs for the dining table in this house. Whether you strike gold or challenge yourself to integrate something old but pretty into your new space, the basement or other storage areas can be magical places.

We're big fans of getting creative and incorporating old things that you find in your house into your decor, especially if the stuff would otherwise be thrown away. Maybe you'll turn some ancient vent covers into wall art, or use those weird green tiles you found in a box as accents in your bathroom. In the Old Meets New House, we saved a bit of the burnt wallpaper from one of the bedrooms.

In a frame, the ombre pattern of soot, ash, and smoke makes you look twice—it could be a solar system or a skyline. You never know when something someone else might consider trash could become a favorite object in your home.

WAIT FOR THE MOMENT

This tip may not be super helpful for those who are trying to cut down on impulse buys, but a few of the most impactful pieces in the Old Meets New House were unplanned splurges, or purchased well before we even had a place to keep them, much less knew where we would use them.

The mantel was one of several salvaged from some townhouses in Corktown; we held on to the last one just in case. We found a very special door that we just knew was perfect for this place years before we were ready to put one in (it was also taller and wider than the existing door opening, which leads us to another tip—measure first). We weren't even really looking for a transom window for this space, but Kyle saw one in an antique store and knew it would fit perfectly. The very special, almost iridescent light fixture that now hangs in the main stairway was found in another shop and was initially very much not for sale, but Bo went back and charmed the owner.

The point is, it can pay off to wait for the perfect time to use a very unique object, or keep your mind open while you're shopping to make way for unanticipated moments in your space that might just make it sing.

ABOVE: In many ways renovating this house was an exercise in restraint. Each room presented an opportunity to use reclaimed materials in polished, modern ways—our Modern Bar Cart, made with offcuts from the warehouse, is a great example.

ABOVE RIGHT: The kitchen is truly the heart of this home, and the reclaimed wall-cladding covering built-in storage and the fridge is a huge part of that.

OPPOSITE: A view of the Old Meets New House living room, including a mantel salvaged from a townhouse in Corktown, Detroit, and a few Woodward Throwbacks tables made from reclaimed flooring.

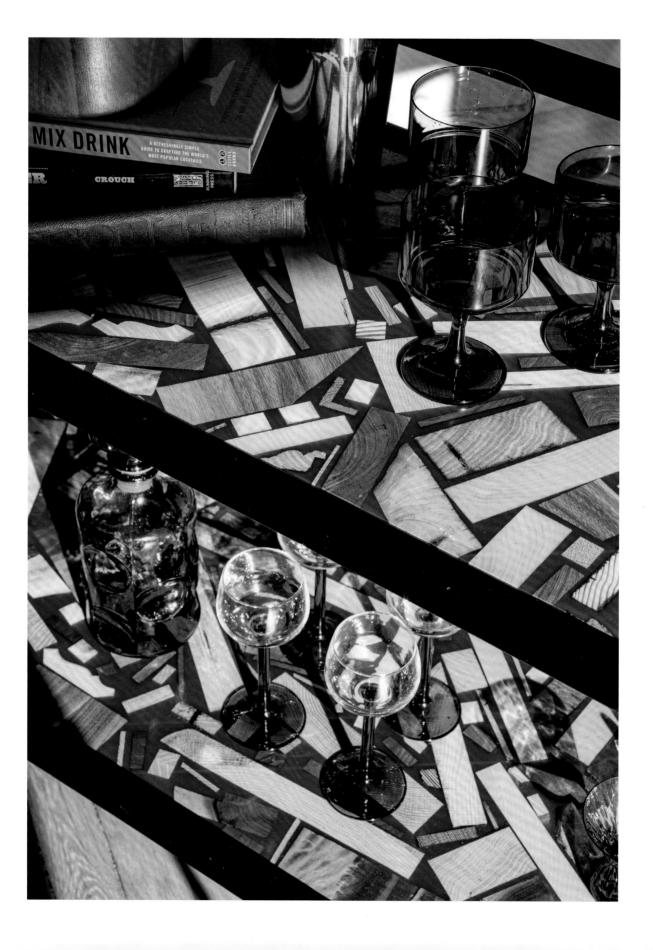

Q + A WITH BO + KYLE

Q: WHAT ARE SOME OF THE BIGGEST LESSONS YOU LEARNED FROM RENOVATING THIS HOUSE?

A: We know this is a very common takeaway, but . . . contractors, contractors, contractors. Who you work with is so important. One of the most painful examples in this house: we had to get rid of the original coved ceilings, which were part of what made us fall in love with it. Initially the contractors said they could work with them, but in the end, they couldn't. Architectural details like coved ceilings are rare today for a reason: they're hard to do, and not many craftsmen still know how to replicate them. Renovating an entire home is really, really hard—when a house is down to the studs, it's overwhelming, and having so much to deal with can make the whole process less enjoyable at times.

But, on a more positive note . . . we did find a lot of cheaper alternatives to more expensive materials, which helped us achieve the look we wanted in our space. Examples include the tile we used for the shower and the backsplash in the kitchen. They have the sheen and organic variation of Zellige tiles, but we got them from Daltile for a fraction of the price. For the kitchen counters, instead of soapstone, we used salvaged phenolic resin, often used for science lab tables. Sometimes people get too caught up in the hype when there are less expensive options that will have similar impact.

Q: WHERE DID YOU START IN TERMS OF THE DESIGN?

A: Our starting point, as always, was creating a sleek and modern design with salvaged materials. At first, we were planning to live in this space, so we were designing for ourselves and pretty much let our imaginations run wild. Eventually, plans changed and we decided to sell, so we had to take into consideration that it wouldn't be us living here. There's a sweet spot between appealing to a wide audience and the house having personality, and the materials we love are not always to everyone's taste. There were a few things we had to tone down because they would have been a little too wild, like the idea of using wood instead of tile for the backsplash in the kitchen, or installing a crazy rusted, paint-chipped, salvaged mantel for the fireplace in the living room.

Q: WHAT WAS THE HARDEST PART OF THIS PROJECT?

A: The hardest part was letting it go! For a long time, we weren't sure if we were going to live here or not, and the more time and effort we put into it, the more attached we got. In the end, it made the most sense to find a very special owner who would appreciate all the love we've put into it and use this space to build our brand as serious interior designers. Now it's time to get started on the next project!

Q: WHAT'S ONE DETAIL YOU WANT PEOPLE TO NOTICE IN THIS SPACE?

A: We hope people look down and notice the flooring. There are several kinds of flooring here, and a lot of work went into all of them—from the refinished original wood in the first-floor hall and kitchen to the floor upstairs, which was salvaged from a school gym. We weren't able to save the floor in the living room, which had been super warped by a water leak, but we kept all we could to create some pieces in our line of furniture made from wood flooring, and then installed reclaimed flooring from a house in Birmingham, Michigan, instead. These are the kind of details that some people might just walk past—or over—but for us, and hopefully for the people who live here, the quality and the history will matter.

None of the floors in this house are perfect—you can see the age and the places we patched it—but honestly, we think totally immaculate flooring is overrated. Embrace the patches, stains, and scratches—they tell the story of all your house has been through.

FLOORING

Flooring is a tactile experience, but this intimate daily contact between foot and floor—textured or smooth, shiny or worn, warm or cold—is often overlooked. Beyond that classic renovation story of peeling back carpet or linoleum hoping for perfect hardwood, you might not give your floors that much thought. But the texture, material, and colors of your floors have a huge impact on your space, and can speak to your house, its history, and your lifestyle. We've worked on so many houses that were total gut jobs, so we appreciate what it means to have floors that you can walk across without putting shoes on. Maybe that's why we have so much value for this part of the home.

We're all about working with the floors you have if you can—yes, even if that means you're embracing linoleum, or maybe even (gasp) painting your hardwood if it's beyond refinishing. If we are installing new flooring, we want the materials we use to have a story if possible.

Floors are a great opportunity to use salvaged materials. Especially in an old space, a floor made from older materials feels authentic to a house's story, and older wood or tile often has better grain and texture—it feels more lived in. Or, flooring can become something else if it has to be replaced; for example, we love using old floorboards to make furniture in our Wood Flooring collection.

A few of the older houses in this book have beautiful, unique, patterned tile entryways, which show the wealth and thought that used to go into this part of the house. We like to think about floors the same way—as precious architectural elements rather than something that's meant to blend in.

ABOVE: Some see trash, others see treasure. These salvaged floorboards sit in our warehouse waiting for their moment to be transformed into something beautiful.

OPPOSITE: The floors in the Dreamy House were too thin to refinish, so the owners decided to paint them. The all-white look ends up being one of the most distinctive parts of this home.

The rich brown concrete floor in the Forge House adds polish and warmth to this textured and industrial space.

We think linoleum gets a bad rap. Just look at the pattern, colors, and texture!

There are two examples of flooring here: the actual floor salvaged from a home in metro Detroit, and an end table made with old flooring from the Old Meets New House.

Many older homes in Detroit boast beautiful, intricately tiled entryways.

Polished concrete is a durable and easy-to-maintain flooring solution. Here it acts as a simple, solid anchor for the airy and bright Garage House.

THE DREAMY HOUSE

W e were in for a surprise when we stepped through the front door of this relatively unassuming American Foursquare-style house on Detroit's East Side. With a warm, all-white color palette, plentiful natural light streaming in through the windows, and beautiful, unique objects artfully displayed everywhere you look, this place feels like a serene oasis. It's the kind of aspirational space that immediately makes you dream of living there—hence the name, the Dreamy House. It's minimal, while still feeling homey and intimate—the result of a thoughtful and meticulous renovation that preserved and added so much personal character.

Owners Christina and Stephen spent a long time searching for a house with some original details intact—and saw a lot of homes that had been through play-it-safe, cheap facelifts in the process. After finally finding this 1907 house with original floors, trim, and doors, they spent just as much time selecting materials and furniture that make the home truly their own. They salvaged and reused wherever they could, made the best of some renovation snafus, and indulged in a few splurges where they'd really pack a punch. Intelligent design decisions and carefully chosen materials and objects make this space unique and unforgettable, worlds away from a typical, gray, plain Jane house flip.

FAVORITE MOMENTS

Let's start with the beautiful staircase that greets you when you come through the front door. The red oak of the posts, balustrades, and handrails is unpainted; the rich, warm wood and well-worn texture are a beautiful contrast to the white paint the owners chose for the walls, floors, and trim.

Looking up, a long, sculptural lamp floats down from the second floor to the entryway. Designed by iconic artist and architect Isamu Noguchi, the lamp is a great example of an intentional splurge placed for maximum impact. The relatively simple white shade complements the unfussy minimalism of the rest of the house, while also introducing a rough and wrinkly texture. A super ornamental chandelier wouldn't make sense here, but the scale and setting of this more minimal lamp still make an impression, and the contrasting heights, spaces, colors, and shapes are a perfect introduction to the home.

Walk a few steps through the entryway and you'll see the true star of the house: the deep-red, almost purple marble used for the kitchen countertop and backsplash. This material is a real keystone for the space (more on that later)—but first: Can we talk about the shelf above the backsplash?

A special material like this marble calls for special objects, and the art, curios, and knickknacks here are both useful and pretty: cherished teacups and glassware bought from antique stores; brass candlesticks purchased for Christina and Stephen's wedding; and paintings, wood, and stoneware found on or inspired by the couple's travels. Altogether these personal, curated, and homey touches tone down the drama of the marble, so the gorgeous, colorful stone looks like it was meant to be there, even in the middle of the house's otherwise minimal white-and-wood palette.

SNAG THE STYLE

We keep using words like *personal* and *unique* to describe this home, and that's because the owners paid such close attention to the objects and materials they chose to fill it. If there's one thing to take away from the Dreamy House, it's that if you surround yourself with pieces, colors, shapes, and textures that you love, things that feel like you, the result is usually magic.

OPPOSITE: Talk about a showstopping moment. The modern lines of the light fixture, designed by Isamu Noguchi, contrast wonderfully with the more traditional millwork in this space.

DESIGN AROUND ONE MATERIAL

When they were house-hunting, Christina and Stephen knew the kitchen was the one room that they'd want to give a complete overhaul, regardless of the home they eventually bought. Sometimes a room that's a total gut job can be the toughest to design, but the homeowners found a secret weapon when they picked their marble. Letting the stone's bold color speak for itself made it easier for them to make decisions about the rest of the space.

In the kitchen, white oak cabinets and other relatively minimal wood and white elements balance out the deep-red stone. The same warm, earthy, sunlit palette continues throughout the house, tying the space together. The more you look, the more

marble, stone, and earthenware you'll see, from pitchers, jugs, vases, and sculptures, to tabletops and counters. These keystone elements add weight, color, and texture to the otherwise bright rooms.

Maybe in your space, instead of marble, you'll design around leather or a special salvaged tile, or the aesthetic of a statement piece of art will influence the palette of the rest of your home. Whether it's the pattern of a vivid wallpaper on an accent wall or your collection of old quilts, choosing a favorite color, material, or object to build a house around can help you create a thoughtful, cohesive interior when you don't know where to begin.

SAVE THE SCRAPS

Ready to talk about marble some more? Good, because in this house, this material deserves some extra attention. Upstairs, two slabs of light pink marble on dowel-covered pedestals serve as a coffee table, and in the awesome primary bathroom, pieces of eye-catching green marble are used as a vanity.

What do these pieces have in common, besides the marble theme? They're both DIY. Christina and Stephen cleverly used marble remnants (leftover offcuts that are too small or weirdly shaped to use in most spaces) to create these surfaces, now centerpieces of their home.

Because beautiful materials like these (not just marble but also textiles, a spare box of tile, and special scrap wood, to name a few) are usually discarded, you can often find them at a huge discount, or even free. With a little creativity and elbow grease, you can transform these materials into one-of-a-kind furniture or art that sparks conversation.

OPPOSITE: In this upstairs sitting room, rustic and polished pair perfectly, from the all-white walls, floors, and trim to the DIY coffee tables made from marble remnants.

LEFT: The house's warm palette—mostly creamy white with pink and green accents—continues to the primary bathroom. A chandelier made by Paris-based Astier Ceramics—an antique store find—adds a refined, slightly feminine contrast.

In the kitchen and dining area, every material, color, and piece of decor is carefully chosen, creating a room that feels cohesive, comforting, and totally personal.

Q + A WITH STEPHEN AND CHRISTINA

Q: WHAT INSPIRED THE DESIGN OF THIS SPACE?

A: In the kitchen, we started with the purple marble—it felt like the rest of the design kind of fell into place from there. But beyond that, we are always inspired by travel and the places we've been. We've spent time in Italy, Amsterdam, and L.A., and those experiences are reflected throughout the space—we love the all-white interiors of Italian homes, accentuated by the beauty of the landscape outside the windows. We also love the fun accents, colors, and patterns of Scandinavian and Danish design, and incorporating art by local artists from places we've lived. Even the marble in the kitchen has a connection to a location. Stephen used to work at the Merchandise Mart in Chicago, and we found the marble there.

Q: HOW DO YOU TWO APPROACH DESIGNING TOGETHER? WHAT STRENGTHS AND WEAKNESSES DO EACH OF YOU BRING TO THE PROCESS?

A: Luckily, we have similar aesthetics, but one of us (Christina) is more of a maximalist, while the other (Stephen) is a minimalist. One of us is usually pushing more and the other is pushing less.

Christina tends to find the smaller pieces—like glassware, ceramics, and the trinkets decorating our shelves. She's often drawn to something just because she loves the shape or color; sometimes it's only later she learns she actually found something rare or valuable. (One tip for bargain hunters:

if you come across a set of something, like plates or cups, in an odd number, they're often much cheaper than they would be as a full set.)

Stephen serves as the moderating influence; he'll ask, "Where are we going to put that?" He tends to have a vision of what he wants and does a lot of internet searching to find it, keeping a lot of tabs open or bookmarking things he likes, waiting for the right thing to come along. He'll work on the bigger finds, like our chairs (from Amsterdam, found on 1stDibs) and dining table (which we fell in love with in a shop in Copenhagen). Both of these were really deliberate design choices: we wanted a round table, because everything else in the space is rectangular and straight, and leather chairs, to cut back on all the wood in the house.

Q: WHERE DO YOU LIKE TO SHOP?

A: During the pandemic, we had lots of time to source objects for the house. Going to antique stores in the Detroit area, like Park Antiques and Odd Fellows Antiques, became a kind of hobby—sometimes we went shopping a few times a week. Antiquing is a fun outlet—you never know what you're going to find. You may not even buy anything, but there are some objects that are just cool to see, like going to a museum.

We also like sites like Chairish and 1stDibs—stuff there can be expensive, but less so if you're patient. If something has been listed on one of these sites for a while, try making a lowball offer—you might be surprised at how willing sellers are to negotiate.

Q: WHAT ADVICE WOULD YOU GIVE TO SOMEONE RENOVATING A HOME?

A: One piece of advice we'd give is to roll with the punches. There are always things that go wrong with any renovations, but you have to just stick with it. For example, we really didn't want to paint any of the original wood in the house that wasn't

Bye-bye bland, colorless kitchens—the stunning marble in the Dreamy House makes us never want to see plain gray and white in a kitchen again.

already painted, but when we tried refinishing the floors, we were told they were already too thin to do it properly. So we ended up painting the floors white—and we actually love the result.

MARBLE AND STONE

We're pretty obsessed with stone. It's timeless but also rare: some of the materials we come across are no longer quarried, so using them adds instant impact. Like wood, marble and stone are natural materials, so each piece comes with its own unique streaks, shades, and texture, and we love when these singular marks and grain patterns are allowed to shine. It's another opportunity to add more variations of color, more interest.

It's true that these luxurious materials are not the cheapest. In part that's because they're durable and last hundreds of years, which means they have sustainability cred in addition to looking good. Detroit's roaring twentieth-century economy funded the construction of some pretty opulent buildings; there was a time when marble and stone were imported from all over the world to enhance these architectural masterpieces. Luckily, that means sometimes we still get to play with these beautiful materials through salvage and using remnants (offcuts of marble, available pretty much anywhere stone is sold).

So skip the safe granite and quartzite: find a crazy, dramatic, streaky, bold-colored remnant and position it proudly in your kitchen. Mix and match different kinds of marble if you can't find one piece big enough, and see what happens— who really cares about the edges and seams? Add big, unexpected stone sculptures and objects to give that final special sauce to a room. Bring on the busy—that's when the magic happens.

ABOVE: Old slate chalkboards, salvaged from a Detroit public school, lean against the wall in the warehouse, waiting to be repurposed.

OPPOSITE: This beautiful limestone fireplace is one of many original features gracing the Charming House.

These DIY coffee tables are another clever use of marble remnants, purchased from Woodward Throwbacks' Hamtramck warehouse.

The clever use of remnants for the counters in the Renaissance House kitchen creates a sophisticated effect for a fraction of the cost of new marble.

We love the use of distinct—but still cohesive—marble remnants for the counters in the Mosaic House's kitchen.

Weighty and unexpected, this stone sculpture from Japan holds its own in the wood-paneled living room of the Golden Age House.

The kitchen counters in the Old Meets New House look like soapstone, but they're actually made of science lab tabletops, salvaged from a Detroit college that has since closed its doors.

THE RAW AND REFINED HOUSE

The story of this house's kitchen is one of good neighbors, like-minded aesthetics, and successful collaboration. The owner, Eli, got to know and love our work when he lived near the shop in Hamtramck—at that time, he had been living in a converted church. The desire for a more traditional space with enclosed rooms drew him to this 1914 duplex in Poletown East, a neighborhood between Hamtramck and Eastern Market.

The previous owners had been using the duplex as a single-family residence, so the upstairs kitchen had become a makeshift sewing room. Eli hoped to live upstairs and rent out the bottom unit, so the cramped, dated layout of the long-unused kitchen presented a design conundrum. That's when we came into the picture.

This kitchen was a true partnership between designer and client. Eli came to us with a great eye for art, objects, and colors. He shared our love for salvage and old things, and was willing to trust us when we went out on a limb. Maybe as a result of this collaborative process—or because of Eli's own eclectic style—this space ended up with an awesome mixture of eras and aesthetics, modern pops of color next to period details, and textures that run from rough to polished. It's a great example of a look we like to call Raw and Refined—a delicate balance we're always striving for in the furniture and spaces we create.

FAVORITE MOMENTS

The way all the surfaces in the kitchen come together is a perfect statement of purpose for us as designers. The materials here are all salvage, but still functional and beautiful.

Let's start with the kitchen island, which is made completely out of reclaimed wood. The countertops are salvaged science lab tables, and the bottom cabinets are made from metal sheets that were once part of the facade of a great local breakfast spot, Hamtramck Coney Island. When new owners purchased the diner and started to renovate, the original metal facade of the building was revealed: minty green and hand-lettered with the words "Clothing Department Store." We jumped on the chance to secure it. Only a little section of the lettering made it into Eli's cabinets, but even a small taste of this super distressed bit of Hamtramck history adds another layer of visual interest to this space.

We also think the light fixtures here deserve a special shout-out. The owner found the huge, very eighties pendant lamp that hangs in the kitchen on Chairish. (It almost didn't make it here: the cost to ship it from the Netherlands was more than the price of the lamp itself. Luckily, a friend of Eli's was traveling to Amsterdam, and Eli convinced him to check it on his flight home.) This postmodern lamp provides an awesome contrast with the rustic wood of the island and retro-looking fridge, but also rhymes with all the curves in the space: the arch we installed over the counters, the perfect showcase for all the beautiful Zellige tiles made by Clé, and the rounded edges of the opening between the kitchen and dining room.

Eli found the more traditional light over the dining table at Eastern Market Antiques for a quarter of the price of similar ones he saw online. This beautiful fixture feels like Detroit: it's authentic to the period the house was built, a time when the city's economy was booming and all that wealth was being celebrated in its architecture and design. And it's a great complement to the much more modern lamp in the kitchen.

Fun fact: neither of the ceiling medallions are original; the owner installed them on the advice of a psychic, who said these decorative elements would be very important in this space. We haven't quite heard that one before, but we love the outcome. The way these traditional pieces of trim mix with more modern details nearby is another great

example of how this house seamlessly blends the old and new.

SNAG THE STYLE

While redesigning this kitchen, we learned a lot about restructuring the layout of a space and bringing together the new and old with an amazing color palette.

OPEN SOME DOORS

Not only was Eli's kitchen not being used as a kitchen when he bought his duplex, but the original room was designed for 1914 needs and preferences, which were very different from what we want out of a kitchen today. That was part of the challenge of reconfiguring this space: it was hard to fit in

This shot takes in everything that makes the kitchen sing—the custom island made of wood reclaimed from church pews, countertops made from salvaged lab tables, cabinets made from an old building facade, and more modern and polished elements like the shiny Zellige tile backsplash and statement post-modern light fixture.

One more door of note: we had a little fun with the door to the bathroom off the kitchen. Bo had the idea to replace the upper panel of the original door with salvaged textured glass, and asked an artist friend, Zach Yarrington, to hand-letter the word "Private" on it. This adds a whimsical touch while also adding light into the bathroom.

EVERY COLOR NEEDS A NEUTRAL

The sophisticated mix of bold hues and contrasting neutrals in this space took a lot of fine-tuning to get right. The owner of this house loves vibrant color, a preference that led to a little design back-and-forth (and not only because Bo typically favors black and other darker shades). It was also very important to us that the original color of the old metal sign we used to make the cabinets—a very subtle, light green—didn't get lost among the louder hues.

We picked a moody dark blue for the kitchen, but balanced it out with the bright arch over the lower cabinets, shiny Zellige tiles, and white, retro-inspired appliances. This makes the colorful accents that Eli chose to display on the open shelf—beautiful glass, stoneware, and ceramics—really pop. The inside of the archway between the kitchen and dining room is painted a playful pink, and more pink stands out in the film posters (for some of Eli's films, including *The Famous Joe Project* and *Hard Decisions*) and paintings in the dining room, especially next to the elegant, relaxing gray walls. The way bursts of color are carefully balanced with sophisticated neutrals is another example of the Raw and the Refined coexisting in this space.

everything a modern kitchen needs, like essential appliances and room to hang out while cooking. In order to make some space, we ended up moving around some doors.

There had once been two doors on the wall where the refrigerator now is: one leading to a bedroom, the other to the dining room you can now see through the large archway we opened up during the renovation. Ultimately, replacing the doors with an archway was a quick and relatively inexpensive fix to both give us more wall space in the kitchen and make it feel more connected to the adjacent dining area. Eli wanted a social kitchen where people could hang out and chat while he cooked and cleaned up, and replacing the doors with an archway allowed much more communication between both rooms.

OPPOSITE: A poster for one of the owner's movies, *Hard Decisions,* adds the perfect amount of pink to the dining area.

LEFT: A closer look at the kitchen island—the reclaimed wood has a texture that can't be faked.

A view from the dining area into the kitchen; art by C Finley, and woven basket planters made by Detroit-based company Love Travels. Imports.

The Raw and Refined House's dining area contrasts with the kitchen in its lighter color palette and more traditional decor. The antique table is a favorite Craigslist find; the pendant lamp, found in an antique shop, is accentuated by a period-appropriate ceiling medallion installed by the house's owner.

Q + A WITH ELI

Q: HAVE YOU ALWAYS LOVED SALVAGED OBJECTS AND MATERIALS?

A: I lived in New York from the late 1990s to the early 2000s, so my aesthetic is very New York loft in the nineties—that mix of industrial with Gilded Age detail, lots of reclaimed stuff, using things for another purpose than what they were made for. This was before bedbugs were as big of a problem, so furniture I found on the street was a big part of how I furnished my apartment. To me, that's just the best way to decorate—with stuff that already exists. There are obvious advantages to reusing when it comes to home design, but I also think older materials and objects just look more interesting. I just think they're beautiful.

Q: TELL US ABOUT THE PROCESS OF WORKING WITH BO AND KYLE ON YOUR KITCHEN.

A: I contacted Bo and Kyle because I just couldn't visualize how to make this space into a kitchen—I know how to decorate a space, but redoing the layout was totally beyond me. Once we started working together, there honestly wasn't too much back-and-forth, because I literally love everything that Bo and Kyle do. Essentially, our process consisted of them showing me their design, me saying, "Oh, I don't know, maybe that's not a good idea," and them saying, "No, that really is a good idea," and me saying, "Okay." And everything truly worked out—like, I already loved Zellige tiles, so when they suggested using that for the backsplash, it confirmed my decision to work with them.

Q: WHAT ARE SOME OF YOUR FAVORITE OBJECTS IN THIS SPACE?

A: There are a few objects in here that I bought just because I loved the way they looked, but then ended up being some of my favorite things in the house. One example is the donabe pots on the open shelf in the kitchen—they're Japanese pots used mainly for cooking rice and making soup, and I thought I would just put them on display. But it turns out I actually use them all the time. They're so functional, and great for heating up leftovers.

Something similar happened with the dining table—I had actually gone to a storage unit to look at something else I'd found on Craigslist, but I loved the table so much that I bought it even though it didn't make any sense for my space. I used to spend much more time hanging out on the couch than sitting at the table, but now that's totally flipped—I love hanging out at this table.

I also need to mention the twisty piece of metal on the white table in the corner of the dining room—that piece actually came from the building's original water heater. I think it was used to stir up the water when it was being heated. I saw it when we were throwing it away, and just thought it was a beautiful object. I'd love to find a better way to display it.

Q: WHAT DO YOU LOVE ABOUT DETROIT?

A: My neighborhood is a huge reason why I moved here. The particular block that I'm on is a great community; a lot of my neighbors have been here a long time, and there are lots of artists and artisans. There's a huge, open, shared space in the middle of the block that we call the Back 40—it's essentially a giant community garden and greenspace, and we even flood it to make an ice-skating rink in the winter. It's the kind of thing that's hard to imagine in any other city. There's something a little storybook about it.

I also just love driving around Detroit and seeing the old hand-lettered signs, the old buildings. So the fact that I get to have the cabinets in my kitchen made out of an old facade from Detroit is a huge treat for me.

THE RAW AND REFINED HOUSE

DOORS

We like to think of doors not only as objects but also as experiences: things you're going to touch and feel, how you're going to travel from one room to another. The cooler the door, the cooler the experience, and there are so many different, amazing doors. (Trust us, we know: if you took a peek inside our warehouse, you might think we were door hoarders.)

Doors can be made of metal; they can have rad features, like beautiful glass or hardware; they can tell stories with texture or indications of past use. Typically, the more panels, the rarer the door—you don't see six- or eight-panel doors as often as you see two-panel ones.

But really, there are no rules; fitting something crazy or handmade into your space can be magic, and older doors are just as functional as new doors, if not more so. There's also a lot you can do to elevate a door if you're not planning on switching it out. You can paint, repaint, or let the natural wood or old paint job show through; you can find new hardware to make a door pop. Most antique shops are full of cool, relatively inexpensive knobs and door plates, so hardware is often an easy gateway into salvage.

In our opinion, the only kind of door that's a bummer is a flat, hollow, slab door. It's a missed design opportunity, and there's no easier way to bring down a room.

One last note: a door doesn't always even have to be a door. Sometimes, an opening or an archway can be just as special or better. Especially when adorned with curved edges, plaster details, or corbels, these portals can make just moving from one room to another memorable.

ABOVE: A treasure trove of door handles in the Woodward Throwbacks warehouse.

OPPOSITE: An Art Deco–style door made by the owner of the Forge House.

In the Raw and Refined House, we transformed an original door by adding cloudy, antique glass and painting "Private" to indicate that it leads to a bathroom.

The Dreamy House's owners widened the doorway leading to their primary suite to install double doors. The dramatic bronze door plates are from an old theater—purchased from the Woodward Throwbacks warehouse.

Dark, solid oak and leaded glass create a totally grand door experience in the Golden Age House.

The stunning original doors in the Golden Age House are a historic homeowner's dream. A coat of green paint makes them feel a hint more 21st-century.

In the main bathroom of the Old Meets New House, a carriage door salvaged from a turn-of-the-century house in Detroit's Indian Village encloses a laundry area.

TRADITIONAL

EACH OF THE TRADITIONAL HOMES FEATURED HERE boasts at least one badass architectural detail that would make any homeowner swoon. Old trim, old doors, leaded glass, built-ins, transom windows—these are special features that take care and effort to build, and you don't see them as often in newer houses. In each of the homes in this section, what we come back to again and again is preserving these traditional details and then figuring out how to decorate with and around them. When these stately spaces are filled with modern and funky objects, the result is some unique and unforgettable contrasts and combinations that really catch the eye—and that's what makes them Throwbacks Homes.

THE GOLDEN AGE HOUSE

Welcome to Boston-Edison—an iconic Detroit neighborhood just north of downtown named for two of its main streets (Boston Boulevard and Edison Avenue). With more than nine hundred homes, it's one of the largest historic residential districts in the country. Most of the homes here were built over a hundred years ago, and they range from relatively simple dwellings to straight-up mansions, a hodge-podge of Tudors, Greek Revivals, Colonials, and more. It's the kind of place where you want to see what's inside, so we feel lucky to have been able to explore this stunning 1906 home.

A who's who of Detroiters have lived in Boston-Edison, from politicians and auto execs to Motown founder Berry Gordy and boxer Joe Louis. This house has its own cool tie to old Detroit: it once belonged to Frank Navin, who owned the Detroit Tigers for much of the early twentieth century. The inside, covered all over with beautiful quarter-sawn oak trim and paneling, is yet another tribute to Michigan history: lumber was the state's biggest industry before automobiles took over. Combined with the eclectic style of current owners Travis and Victoria, this house is an absolute stunner.

Of all the homes in this book, we think this one will make the preservationists happiest. It's a tribute to the Golden Age of Detroit—to the industries that made it wealthy, the figures who made it famous, and the creatives who live here today, honoring the city's history while making it very much their own.

FAVORITE MOMENTS

We have lots of favorite moments in this house. First, we love the disco ball and the neon light in the shape of a camera, perfectly placed in the living room, probably the home's most spectacular space. In the context of all the rich, dark wood paneling that covers so much of this house, these more modern vintage finds are cheeky and unexpected. Sources of light, both literally and figuratively, these shiny, reflective

133

This view from the dining room into a unique, oval-shaped sitting room shows the contrast between the house's original wood trim and trim in the dining room, which has been dripped in a head-to-toe green (Secret Garden by Sherwin Williams).

In the living room, a few different light sources interact with the house's signature dark beams and paneling: the filtered natural light from the leafy backyard; an original, schoolhouse-esque pendant; and of course, a disco ball.

objects brighten up a space that could otherwise be dark and gloomy, and create different moods throughout the day, depending on whether the sun is shining through the windows or the neon light is glowing in the evening. This is a perfect example of how Travis and Victoria haven't been intimidated by their home's well-preserved history and elegant craftsmanship. By boldly mixing their own eclectic style with their house's good bones, they're giving it a second (or maybe third? or fourth?) life.

We also love the way the owners have made their home's grand staircase their own. Generously wide and made of the same impressive wood as the trim and ceiling beams, the stairs are a centerpiece of the house, with unique curved and geometric railings that are almost Art Deco, surprisingly modern for the time they were built. Many people might feel a bit intimidated decorating this beautifully designed and built architectural feature, but you can really feel Travis and Victoria's personality here. A deep landing is the perfect habitat for a bunch of houseplants, which clearly love the light coming from the massive leaded glass window. And irreverently placed contemporary art plays with the staircase's grandeur, from the sculpture at the foot of the stairs—a portrait of Snoop Dogg made by Paige Wright—to the large painting of two bears by artist Blaine Fontana, peeking out over the top of two railings. It's another example of the personal and unexpected making this old, traditional house sing.

SNAG THE STYLE

Finding a home as old as this one in a city that has been through as much as Detroit is pretty rare, so our biggest takeaways here are about preserving all that history. But there are many things in this

OPPOSITE: The Golden Age House's monumental staircase could easily intimidate an interior designer, but irreverent artwork and some happy houseplants make this stately architectural feature feel personal and approachable.

house to inspire, even if you haven't just bought a turn-of-the-century mansion.

IF IT AIN'T BROKE, DON'T FIX IT

After a year of house-hunting, Travis and Victoria had seen enough linoleum covering hardwood floors, and trim that had been repainted over and over again, to know that this relatively untouched house was really special. God knows that over the course of hundreds of salvage jobs and home projects, we've definitely witnessed too many home-reno horror stories to mention. In most cases, people with good intentions make cheap changes to their homes for the sake of convenience or a recent fad. The lesson of Travis and Victoria's house is that with a little foresight, irreversible alterations to historic homes like this one can be avoided.

In a bathroom upstairs, the walls are covered in a tiger motif hand-painted by artist Zach Yarrington.

We're the first to say there are limits to preservation: the amount of labor involved, money, practicality, and personal style preferences are just a few things that might lead you to make a major change to an old home rather than choosing restoration. But Travis and Victoria value all their original hardwood, and intend to keep the more traditional layout of their house, even if it means they won't have a trendy, open-concept kitchen.

We hope that if you're in the market for an older house, it's because you're into all the antique stuff, too. If you're not, maybe a historic home isn't for you, and you should leave all that dark wood trim for someone who'll love it!

At the very least, if you're lucky enough to have original details in your home, please think before altering them forever. They're often impossible to replace, either because the materials are one of a kind or because there aren't many artisans left who know how to replicate them. We've found that when homeowners mix a room's original features with their own unique style, the result is often magical.

MIX AND MATCH

Travis and Victoria respect their old house. But what makes this space for us is that it doesn't feel bogged down by all the history in its furnishings and decorating. Sure, you can furnish your house with authentic period pieces. Or you can try to mix in your own style and see what happens.

The bones of the Golden Age House are an awesome Frankenstein of styles—the staircase has an Art Deco feel; the attention to detail on all the wall treatments is very Craftsman; ornamental wood columns reference Neoclassical architecture. But those terms don't describe any of the furniture or art inside. Geometric pottery and stylish houseplants line old built-in shelves; bright, modern art is hung on the walls; contemporary light fixtures pop in the dining room, painted dark green. The furniture is mostly Mid-century Modern, but with the odd eclectic object, like a very heavy stone Japanese tea lamp, thrown in.

This home feels lived in, and like it represents the people who live here. The art, furniture, and objects, from a variety of periods and aesthetics, range from hand-me-downs to antique-fair finds, but what they have in common is that at some point Travis and Victoria fell in love with them and found just the right spot to put them. We think any homeowner can achieve their very own mix-and-match style if they just listen to their intuition rather than simply try to match their house's built-in aesthetic.

The dining room was one of the homeowners' biggest projects to date. They updated the lighting with fixtures from STUFF by Andrew Nayer and took the risk of painting the original hardwood an on-trend green, which offers such a nice contrast with the original wood in the adjoining sitting room.

An only-in-an-old-house surprise: The paneling in this sitting room conceals a secret bar cabinet, which probably came in handy during Prohibition.

Q + A WITH TRAVIS AND VICTORIA

Q: WHY DETROIT?

A: People often try to compare Detroit to other cities, but we think Detroit has its own thing going on. Yeah, we can't walk everywhere, and maybe we don't have some of the things that people think of when it comes to a big city. But Detroit has opportunities, like the opportunity to find a house in your budget, or the opportunity to start a business from the ground up. That's not to say it's impossible in other cities, but it's so much more accessible here. It's a city you can really feel a part of.

Q: WHAT DREW YOU TO THIS HOUSE?

A: When we were house-hunting, we weren't necessarily looking for an old home, or a particular architectural style. But we learned so much over a year of looking. We kept running into a choice: Do we want something move-in ready, or do we want something cheap but that would have to be rebuilt from the ground up? After we'd seen a bunch of places, we realized that Detroit fixer-uppers are on another level. We were willing to give a space some TLC, but since we both have full-time jobs, we decided we needed something that was move-in ready.

And when we first looked at this house, we'd looked at so many places that we knew it was special. It had never been through a Home Depot house flip, it had been so well taken care of, and we're only the fourth owners. It was just immaculate. We just feel so lucky that a butterfly effect of things went right for us and we were able to buy it.

Q: HOW WOULD YOU DESCRIBE YOUR STYLE?

A: For the longest time our starting point was Mid-century Modern; we knew that we liked a lot of the furniture that fit into that aesthetic.

But over time we learned more about Detroit architecture and funky styles like Mayan Revival—that's the architectural style of the Guardian Building, which is one of the most beautiful skyscrapers downtown. That aesthetic started to find its way into our style, like in our Southwestern-inspired rugs and pillows. We still love things that have simple, mid-century shapes, but we've gotten funkier, like incorporating a huge Japanese tea lamp that our friends got us into the living room, or adding in a neon light that's shaped like a camera.

It's hard to put our finger on exactly what our style is, but that's kind of why we like it. Our home is really just a collection of things that mean something to us; they don't all have to be the same aesthetic.

Q: WHAT'S YOUR BEST DECORATING ADVICE?

A: Don't rush it! When you first move in, it's easy to feel like you need to get all the "forever things." But you start to look at prices and realize that's just not realistic.

We ended up incorporating a lot of our old stuff into this new house. We've lived in smaller apartments and more industrial-style lofts, and it was cool to see how our furniture looked in a larger,

more traditional home. Some of the pieces really pop with all the dark wood.

Is all the stuff we've reused exactly what we'd want, in a perfect world? Probably not. But it works for now, and over time, we can continue to elevate our style as we find those forever things. Being patient, taking your time, and making shopping for your home more like a treasure hunt, finding perfect pieces bit by bit, can be really fun.

TRIMS AND TREATMENTS

We can't gush enough about the paneling and trim in the Golden Age House (page 133), and we're pretty much obsessed with these original features wherever we find them. Why? Because features like these in houses this old are often irreplaceable. Older materials are usually higher quality than the standard stuff you can find at the lumber yard today, which means re-creating their effect is either crazy expensive or impossible.

By trims and treatments here, we mean the features that spruce up a home's walls, floors, ceilings, and windows, from baseboards to paneling to coffers. These are mostly made of wood, but sometimes you'll be lucky enough to find molding, coved ceilings, or other features made of plaster in older homes. Trims and treatments speak to the history of the home and the time it was made, and make a space magical. So if you're lucky enough to find a place with these original elements, please take good care of them—and if you don't like the way they look, maybe don't buy the house, to save them for someone who does!

Finally, a word on painting trim. For us, this is complicated. Sometimes—and we know some people will hate us for saying this—it can make sense to paint trim, especially if it's lower quality, for a pop of color. If you find trim that's already painted, you should feel free to go to town—in the end, it's your house. But do think twice before altering it or ripping it out—remember, features like these are sometimes impossible to re-create.

OPPOSITE: A sculptural mask in the likeness of Snoop Dogg, made by artist Paige Wright, is the perfect tongue-in-cheek accompaniment to all of the beautiful trim on the staircase of the Golden Age House.

Unpainted trim in the Dreamy House pops against the creamy, all-white palette.

Some may think it's dated, but we can't get enough of the very seventies wall paneling in the basement of the Not Your Grandma's House.

The Renaissance House's trim was not in great shape, but the current owner salvaged just enough of it to create this beautiful moment around a bay window, letting the texture and imperfections show through.

Details like the plasterwork seen here in a doorway in the Charming House are hard to find these days, and they inspire so much respect for the artisans who took the time to make them.

Tin crown molding in the foyer of the Old Meets New House. The original molding was damaged by the fire that put the building in such a precarious state, so we painstakingly replaced it. These aren't the kind of details you ever want to lose.

THE COSMOPOLITAN HOUSE

The owners of this 1920s duplex in Virginia Park—a tiny sliver of a historic district nestled north of downtown—fell in love with it shortly after visiting on a trip from Brooklyn, New York. Given the couple's lifelong interest in design and cosmopolitan sense of style, it's no surprise that their Detroit space is sophisticated, elegant, and well curated.

The main thing that makes this space feel so put together is the bold, monochromatic color palette. The minute you enter the Cosmopolitan House, the teal-green paint that so defines the living and dining rooms is a total mood; entering this space is transportive, like the feeling of diving underwater. It creates the perfect backdrop for owners Tux and Russell to play with in their furniture and art, mixing curated colors, tones, and textures to create an almost Wes Anderson, storybook vibe. This cozy, cultivated space is a truly unique reflection of its owners.

FAVORITE MOMENTS

The placement of art in the living room, and how well it coordinates with the room's color scheme, is definitely a moment. Owners Tux and Russell are very good at picking out art and hanging it in just the right spot. (The awesome original picture rail—a once-common type of trim used to hang art, so you didn't have to put holes in your wall—definitely adds to the effect.)

First, over the fireplace, whose bricks have been painted in Black Knight by Benjamin Moore, hangs a colorful oil painting of a pair of pheasants. There's a variety of colors in the painting, but the warm mustard yellow and this house's signature teal green stick out the most. These colors work together because they're on just about opposite sides of the color wheel. Complementary colors aren't just for art class—they can be a great tool for figuring out how to attractively combine colors. The painting's palette is the perfect complement to the living room's color scheme, with teal-painted trim (Dragonfly, also by Benjamin Moore) inspired by wallpaper the owners chose for the foyer.

We also love that this painting has a Detroit connection—the city is home to a thriving population of pheasants, who love living in the tall grass that grows in many of the vacant lots, so seeing one of these beautiful game birds is not uncommon.

A second example of skillfully chosen, perfectly placed art is the portrait hung smack-dab in the middle of two gorgeous leaded glass windows over a plush yellow couch. The mixture of colors, textures, and materials just plain pleases the eye, and makes you want to linger for a while.

Our other favorite corner of this house is a baller credenza that the owners found in an antique store in Ypsilanti, Michigan. Though it looks mid-century, it's actually from the eighties, which kind of explains the awesome, extra moody smoked glass. The drama really turns up in the evening—the interior of the credenza can be lit, illuminating Tux and Russell's curated collection of glassware. A showstopping piece like this can really set the tone for a space—the muted light filtered through the glasses and vases contributes to the house's atmospheric, aquatic feel.

SNAG THE STYLE

Tux and Russell's house offers some great inspiration for developing your own personal style.

COLOR STORY

The Cosmopolitan House is blessed with some amazing original features, such as century-old doors and lovely leaded glass. But over the course of tenants coming in and out and years of wear,

this space has inherited a variety of old-house problems, including trim that had become thick and gummy from countless coats of paint. Tux and Russell turned this common historical renovation issue into an opportunity, starting fresh with the bold teal paint that so characterizes this space.

There's a lot to be said for going all in on a bold color you love throughout your house. Working within a limited palette can actually be freeing, offering tons of opportunities to play complementary and contrasting hues against the dominant one. In the Cosmopolitan House, a great example of this is a set of mustard-yellow, gingham chairs that really pop next to the teal-green paint. (These

Some pieces from two of the owners' collections: glassware and portraiture (especially with feminine subjects).

chairs were one of Tux and Russell's first purchases for the home; they bought them before they even had a place in mind to put them.) The vibey color contrast contributes to the fairy-tale, almost cinematic aesthetic of the space.

We also love the way a room looks when walls, ceiling, and trim are all painted one color, like in Tux and Russell's dining room. If you're hesitating about painting your ceiling, we think this room is proof that this luxurious and classic look totally works. Just make sure to use matte on the walls and ceiling and semi-gloss on the trim; this will add richness and depth to the color rather than making it feel flat and one-dimensional.

BE ON THEME

Look around the Cosmopolitan House and themes start to emerge everywhere, even beyond the synchronized color scheme. The first thing you might notice is a repeating pattern in the art: there are a lot of portraits, most of them with feminine subjects. (Tux and Russell found many of them through Goodwill's online store, which is one of their favorite overlooked decor sources.) We love the way building a collection like this creates a through line in a house. In keeping with the theme of iconic women, they even have a few votive candles paying tribute to Joumana, a Detroit-area lawyer whose many massive billboards have made her a local celebrity. Look closely and you'll spot a few other collections here: for example, Tux and Russell clearly have a thing for piggy banks, and their beautiful assortment of glassware is another highlight. Starting to collect is also a fun way to give some direction to your antiquing adventures.

OPPOSITE: Looking into the dining room from the living room, it's easy to see how these two areas complement each other while still having their own unique feel.

ABOVE: A colorful bookshelf, complete with some pieces from the owners' delightful collection of piggy banks.

Sometimes called "color-drenching," the technique of using the same color of paint for the walls, ceiling, and trim is extra dramatic when a room boasts the beautiful molding seen here in the Cosmopolitan House.

Q + A WITH TUX + RUSSELL

Q: WHAT BROUGHT YOU TO DETROIT?

A: We visited Detroit for the first time in the summer of 2021 and completely fell in love. It's just such a great city. The food and bar scene, the art and music and nightlife, the history and the architecture, and the feeling of restoration and growth and excitement in the air made Detroit feel ideal on so many levels. We returned home saying we could see ourselves living here.

Within three days after our trip, we found this house online, and by the next weekend, we had booked another flight to come see it. We were obsessed with the leaded windows and crown moldings. There is also so much going on in this neighborhood—so many of our neighbors are working on their houses like we are, and we love being able to walk to the Congregation, a nearby café housed in a former church.

Q: WHAT WAS YOUR THOUGHT PROCESS WHEN IT CAME TO DECORATING THIS SPACE?

A: We wanted to do something totally different here from our place in Brooklyn, where we didn't really play with color at all; it's all very beigy, gray, and pale neutral. So here we decided we were going to go crazy. We wanted to totally play it up and go super colorful with it.

When it comes to furniture, our style is typically very Mid-century Modern, but since this house is older, we wanted to find some older pieces and have a mix of eras. We didn't want a house from the twenties filled with furniture from the sixties.

Q: WHERE DO YOU FIND YOUR ARTWORK AND FURNITURE?

A: Most of the stuff in here is thrifted from Facebook Marketplace and antique shops. A lot of the art is from Goodwill—they have an online store that you can search by keyword. I found a lot of the portraits in our space by searching keywords like "woman painting." It's sort of our best-kept secret; I almost don't want to tell anyone about it.

We bought some things on sites like Wayfair. If you're doing that, be sure to measure before you buy; sometimes things are photoshopped into rooms in the pictures, and they don't pay attention to scale. Then it's delivered and you open it up and it's way smaller than you thought it would be. We've learned our lesson on that one.

Q: WHAT ADVICE WOULD YOU GIVE TO SOMEONE TAKING ON A FIXER-UPPER?

A: The first couple of months were rough. We were sleeping on a mattress on the floor and using a milk crate that we found in the hallway as a coffee table. We didn't really know anyone yet, and there was so much work to do on the house. With any renovation, there are growing pains—you see the vision, but you have to go through some stuff before it can become a reality.

We also had a lot of help from Tux's mom, who has been just incredible. She fixed up every apartment their family moved into, and we've learned so much from her. It's so meaningful to have that kind of experience and support when you're taking on a project like this.

PAINT

It's a well-known home improvement fact that paint is one of the easiest and cheapest ways to transform a space. Sure, it takes some effort to tape the trim and get a few good, even coats on, but pound for pound no other weekend project can make as big of an impact on your home.

When it came to paint, we historically skewed either neutral or dark and moody—nothing in between. If we were working with pops of color, they were generally baked into the materials we were using, like the old, hand-painted signs that we love or the paint-splattered patina of salvaged scaffolding.

But recent projects we've taken on, like using sherbet-orange paint in a bathroom facelift at the Home Base (page 59), or choosing an elegant crimson color inspired by automotive design on the cabinets in the Loft House (page 47), have challenged and inspired us. And in the homes we visited in this book, paint caught our eye most when it was bright and bold. What we've learned is that if you love a color, don't question it too much, and don't be afraid. You can try it as an accent in your space, and if it doesn't work, don't panic—it's just paint. It can always be redone.

Paint can also inspire controversy among interior design geeks. We've seen people chewed out on social media for painting their original hardwood—and to some extent, we get it. If you're lucky enough to have a beautiful material like that in your home, it can be a shame to alter it. But when it comes down to it, if it's not working for you, we say do what you want. At the end of the day, it's your house. And a fresh coat of paint in a color you love can do a lot to really make it feel that way.

ABOVE: This fun riff on wallpaper with a tiger motif in the Golden Age House is actually hand painted.

OPPOSITE: The Not Your Grandma's House is especially good at going all-in on a color scheme: here, pink on pink (Infatuation by Behr) is broken up with some colorful and brass elements.

The complementary pairing of green (Avocado by Behr) and pink (Infatuation, also by Behr) dominates the whole color scheme of the Not Your Grandma's House.

Bo usually gravitates toward darker colors, but she challenged herself to use Golden Mist by Benjamin Moore in the Home Base powder room revamp. The contrast between black trim and hardware, deep-green sink, and warm wall paint works great here.

In the moody powder room in the Old Meets New House, dark green paint (Chimichurri by Benjamin Moore) is accentuated by low ambient lighting and matte black sink and fixtures.

The paint used for the cabinets in the Loft House was color-matched from a paint swatch Bo got from an auto shop.

The built-ins in the dining room of the Golden Age House look great in a fresh coat of green paint (Secret Garden by Sherwin-Williams).

THE CHARMING HOUSE

The quirky East English Village neighborhood, situated on Detroit's eastern border, is full of architectural diversity. When this area was being developed—mostly in the 1930s, during the Great Depression—the homeowners themselves, rather than contractors, hired builders and custom-ordered the details for their homes. The resulting hodgepodge of styles and eras means the Throwbacks Home mix-and-match aesthetic is baked right into the neighborhood.

This house is a Tudor, an architectural style inspired by medieval England, and though it's not particularly large, the luxurious attention to detail makes it feel like a fairy-tale castle. But where Tudor houses are often dark, this one is filled with light coming through amazing, almost Art Deco windows with colorful, bubbled leaded glass. Tiled windowsills and coved ceilings give this home classic New York, almost subway, vibes. A very extra Detroit Pink Bathroom feels seventies Hollywood Regency—but nope, it's original. And the plasterwork ranges from ornate to funky, as in the kitchen, where somebody used plaster to replicate the effect of cinderblocks.

There wasn't a lot of extra money going around in the 1930s, so the fact that the builders incorporated all of these elements into the house makes it pretty special. You get the sense that whoever designed the home had a huge imagination and was letting it run wild, and we love that the current owners, Emily and Chris, are honoring and preserving that creativity. Add in an expertly curated collection of antiques, and what do you get? A totally charming, one-of-a-kind Throwbacks Home.

FAVORITE MOMENTS

There are so many great details in this house, but one of our favorite moments is the bathroom, where the goodness is so unexpected, it takes you by surprise. You know that even in a more traditional home, we're going to look for the funky.

The Charming House boasts what the owners call a Detroit Pink Bathroom, which is very much a thing. A certain kind of historic-home aficionado is stoked when they find one of these floor-to-ceiling pink-tiled gems—and we want to get you guys excited about them, too. The uninitiated might look at all that salmon pink and think "dated," but Emily and Chris are dedicated to preserving this piece of Detroit history. In our eyes, this time-capsule bathroom is as beautiful as it is functional, from the elegant archways over the separate tub and shower to the original Art Deco light fixtures.

The mirror behind the tub is unique: etched into the glass is a swamp scene complete with a crane swallowing a fish. When the owners first bought the place, they thought this funky seventies-looking detail must have been added later, but they have been able to confirm it's original. Emily is the first to say that having a mirror right next to the tub can be a bit awkward, but she wouldn't change a thing about the bathroom, and neither would we—this eccentric, glamorous mirror combines with the more classic details to make this room one of a kind. The moral of the story is, embrace the period. Embrace the pink. When surrounded by the rest of the house's refined, timeless style and antiques, this bathroom doesn't feel dated—it feels like the star of the show. Even if a historical detail in your space isn't exactly what you would have chosen, giving it a chance to interact with your favorite objects and aesthetics can result in some interior design magic.

Another terrific moment is the special hutch in the dining room filled with ceramics handmade by Emily and her mom. It was found on Chairish and is clearly mid-century, but was just unusual enough for a piece from this period to strike Emily's fancy. This unique spin on a Mid-century Modern silhouette goes perfectly with the earthy pottery on display. This corner boasts other details from a mix

of different periods—creamy glass schoolhouse lighting, a more modern-looking brass-and-wood light fixture, and the Eastlake mirror. The proudly arranged ceramics collection and the carefully chosen objects that surround the hutch are a perfect illustration of what works about this space.

SNAG THE STYLE

The main takeaway from the Charming House is to preserve the historic details if you've got them. But here are a few other things we learned from this space.

OPPOSITE: A few of the things that make the Charming House special can be seen here: the fabulous original plasterwork, and perfectly curated antiques (in this case, a unique mid-century hutch, and a beautiful Eastlake-style mirror.

Ladies and gentlemen, we give you:
a Detroit Pink Bathroom.

ANTIQUING 101

There are so many benefits to buying antique, used, and vintage; that's one of the biggest things we took away from the Charming House. Not only is buying old stuff better for the environment, it offers you a chance to own a piece of history that you can't just pick up in a store.

But it takes time to learn how to collect antiques that will work in your space. Emily has definitely put in the work; she loves to spend her weekends antiquing and is a huge fan of the quarter-yearly Michigan Antique Festivals. She also grew up in a nineteenth-century house filled with old stuff curated by her equally antique-loving mom.

Here are some of her tips for helping newbie antiquers catch the bug:

- Spend time exploring your local antique shops and get to know the owners. The more familiar you are with what's on offer, the more you'll know what you like (and what it should cost). Your neighborhood picking community can clue you in on antique events like fairs and pop-ups, where the *really* good stuff is on display.
- Become a collector whether you like old spoons or chairs made by a specific designer. Start looking for the same kinds of objects, styles of art, or things from a certain period. This gives your shopping some direction, and it's fun to be an authority on something.
- Check sites like Facebook Marketplace, eBay, and Craigslist for wild finds at even wilder prices. Even scrolling through Instagram can help you get a sense of silhouettes and aesthetics that you like.

WHAT'S OLD IS NEW AGAIN

We love all the beautiful old things in the Charming House, but like we always say when it comes to interior design, there are no hard-and-fast rules. You know by now that we're not purists about

preservation and buying everything secondhand. And because the period pieces in this space serve as such a great backdrop, the owners are able to seamlessly incorporate some newer pieces.

One example is the antique-looking tapestry made of a wallpaper-like material in the primary bedroom—it's actually from Anthropologie. There's a new sofa in the living room, a new table in the dining room, and though Emily and Chris weren't able to save the original cabinets in their kitchen: the new white-and-cane ones they installed during their renovation fit right in, and have all the convenience and storage space a modern kitchen needs. No judgment here—the benefit of having a great base of high-quality old stuff is that you can mix in new stuff without taking away from the space.

Quirky built-in plaster shelves in the
kitchen are the perfect place for the
owners' cookbook collection.

A tapestry from Anthropologie and quilt from Schoolhouse, complemented by some seriously dreamy light.

Subtle pops of blue in the living room create a serene environment that doesn't distract from killer original features, like plaster molding and a stone fireplace.

Q + A WITH EMILY + CHRIS

Q: WHAT IS YOUR FAVORITE THING ABOUT THIS HOUSE?

A: We love all the unexpected details. You don't think of the thirties being a time when people valued unnecessary ornamentation, so the fact that the bar is so unlikely only makes us love it more.

Q: WHAT HAVE YOU LEARNED FROM RENOVATING AND LIVING IN AN OLDER HOUSE?

A: There are a few compromises we had to make while renovating that still bug us a bit. We had to get rid of the original pink toilet in our Detroit Pink Bathroom because it had cracked beyond repair, and ended up putting in carpeting upstairs because the floor was in terrible shape. But that's okay—those are always things we can fix in the future. And honestly, having a carpet upstairs is pretty cozy, especially in the winter. When you're taking on a project as big as an old house, you have to make compromises sometimes, because you need to live in the space.

Q: WHAT ADVICE WOULD YOU GIVE TO SOMEONE TRYING TO ACHIEVE A SIMILAR LOOK TO THE ONE YOU'VE CREATED IN THIS HOME?

A: Besides going to every antique fair that you can? We find that old photographs are a good, reliable decor item. It's fun to look for old photos at shops and antique shows, but the Library of Congress website is another great resource. They have an incredible collection of photos available to print that add instant atmosphere and allow the art you display to be more personal—for example, we printed out and framed a beautiful old photo of Detroit's Belle Isle Aquarium.

Q: WHAT DO YOU LOVE ABOUT ANTIQUING?

A: We love that you never know what you'll find. There's always the possibility that you'll discover something amazing. Like the hutch Emily got from the Michigan Antique Festival in Davisburg, which was once used in the offices of the *Detroit Free Press*. At first we didn't want to junk it up with all our folders and stuff, but now we get to use this beautiful piece with all its history as her day-to-day desk. The best part is, we have keys to all the cubbies—except one. We're just dying to bust it open and see what's inside. Maybe there's a thousand dollars in there—who knows? That feeling of potentially solving a mystery is what makes antiquing addictive.

OPPOSITE: A favorite piece of the Charming House owners: a hutch once used in the office of the *Detroit Free Press*.

GLASS

Sparkly elements like special windows, mirrors, and glassware are the jewelry of the home. Shiny or iridescent, see-through or opaque, these design gems can interact with light and catch the eye to make rooms feel bigger, brighter, warmer, or more colorful.

Maybe you're lucky enough to have unique original windows or other glass features in your space; they just don't make leaded, beveled, or stained glass the way they used to. But if you keep an eye out, you'll also find beautiful glass objects all over antique stores. Decorating with glass is an opportunity to get a little extra and add some pizzazz, and it can be more DIY than you think. Sure, it may take a bit more effort to install an old door with a beautiful cloudy glass panel, or put in a transom window where there wasn't one before, but doing so can transform an entire space, instantly making it dreamier.

But if you're not quite ready for that kind of project, no worries. Glassware is a fun and relatively easy and inexpensive thing to collect when you're out thrifting, and a colorful set of goblets or cups on a shelf can have a ton of impact, too. Plus, they are practical decor. Those gorgeous mid-century glasses are guaranteed to get compliments when you break them out at your next dinner party.

ABOVE: Elements for a next-level but totally worth it DIY project: install an antique transom to add loads of atmosphere and light.

OPPOSITE: Salvaged stained-glass windows add light and color to the Fire House.

The basement bar in the Not Your Grandma's House is the perfect place to display a glassware collection.

Refined antique glassware looks fresh in almost any space, even against the rough, industrial brick walls of the Loft House.

A playful leaded glass window in the Charming House.

Antique beveled glass in the door leading to the powder room of the Old Meets New House lets in light but still allows for privacy.

Lucite, otherwise known as acrylic glass, is another fun material to use to add light and texture to your home.

THE RENAISSANCE HOUSE

This home is located in Detroit's Southwest area, one of the city's most diverse and vibrant, where you'll find Mexicantown and a five-star view of the Ambassador Bridge to Canada. Both the area and the house feel uniquely Detroit. The neighborhood is homey and industrial at the same time, the kind of place where a community garden thrives within sight of huge freighters sliding up and down the Detroit River. Inside the Renaissance House, polished mixes with paint-chipped, the newly installed looks a hundred years old, and bold and inspired design choices set the stage for one-of-a-kind antiques. Combined, it all makes for a space that we think just couldn't happen anywhere else.

Unfortunately, when this house was bought by its current owner, Chris, it didn't have a lot of original features to preserve. In fact, the turn-of-the-twentieth-century Victorian, which had been turned into a sixplex (yes, six families lived here!) sometime in the 1940s, required a total gut job. But it was important to Chris, a designer-contractor, to bring the old back into this space. He used his keen eye and design savvy to create a home that feels authentic and instantly classic without being stuffy, like it was always meant to look this way. Chris brought this house back to life, restoring it to a shine that might just exceed the space's original glory—which is why we've named it the Renaissance House.

FAVORITE MOMENTS

Let's start with the bay window on the first floor, where the owner turned what could have been an old-house problem into a magical moment. There wasn't much trim in the home worth salvaging

179

when Chris bought it, but instead of writing it all off as a loss, he saved what he could to highlight these four beautiful windows with a view of the garden. The bench for the window seat was found in a house that was set for demolition, and in a stroke of luck it fit in the space perfectly, creating the dreamiest reading nook.

We love that Chris didn't "fix" the trim, so the paint-chipped texture tells the story of long years in this home and all that it's been through. It's a great example of how this space puts a spotlight on the old rather than throwing it away or covering it up, an embrace of aging and glamorous decay that reminds us a bit of the beautifully crumbling architecture of New Orleans. In the rest of the house, he installed new trim complete with original-looking corbels and other great details, and the contrast between polished and timeworn is striking.

Our other favorite moment happens to be in a bathroom, where several peeling sheets of old wallpaper were either left as Chris found them, scraped back like layers of an onion, or painstakingly touched up with custom paint colors hand-mixed from herbs to create a fascinating collage of history, colors, and textures.

The designer and his team have since replicated this unconventional technique, which he calls "fucked-up wallpaper," in other spaces. Making sure the walls are sealed is key; they apply several layers of a clear coat, so even though the age of the materials beneath shows through, the room still feels sleek and easy to clean. The result is a wall that both tells the story of the house and is a piece of art in itself, which perfectly sums up the design philosophy of the Renaissance House.

SNAG THE STYLE

Chris designs and decorates for a living, which means he's willing to go to some length to make old stuff fit into and shine in the spaces he works on. But here are some tips on giving your home the same

timeless feel as the Renaissance House, even if you can't put in quite as many hours of elbow grease.

OUT WITH THE NEW, IN WITH THE OLD

Major renovations were required to convert this house from a sixplex into the single-family space you see today, which meant Chris was working with an almost blank slate when he bought the place.

ABOVE: A view of the Renaissance House's "fucked-up wallpaper" in all its glory.

OPPOSITE: One of our favorite moments in the house: a window seat created from all the old trim that could be salvaged from the home before it was renovated.

But instead of filling his home with brand-new everything, he used salvage and antiques wherever he could, which is what makes the house look like it was well-preserved rather than recently renovated.

The work went beyond making use of the house's salvageable trim for a showstopping moment around the bay window. Chris also added architectural features often missing from newer homes, like ornate corbels decorating doorways, a vintage mantel for the fireplace, antique lighting, and found marble remnants and salvaged cabinets in the kitchen. And of course, the space is filled with killer antique furniture and art.

As with all preservation and salvage jobs, there were some limits. Chris is very good at pivoting by filling the house with things that aren't original but look like they could be. For example, he wasn't able to keep much of the original flooring, because redoing the layout required ripping out most of it. When the original transom windows were damaged by accident, he swapped them out with others he found at antique fairs. Modern conveniences like new kitchen appliances and a more open layout on the first floor, along with Chris's own personal style and great eye, keep the space feeling fresh and classic rather than dated and stuffy.

TRIAL, ERROR, AND ELBOW GREASE

We like this space so much because even with antiques and old stuff, it still manages to have a playful, funky vibe. A big reason for that is how willing Chris is to experiment with the materials and objects in his house. His invention of the "fucked-up

In the Renaissance House, there's a little bit of unexpected texture around every corner.

wallpaper," used to such great effect in the bathroom, is just one demonstration of how Chris goes with a crazy idea and ends up with something totally unique.

Here's another: Chris boiled the awesome salvaged light fixtures in the kitchen until they were rusty, brushed them with a copper brush, then sealed them, to achieve the perfect timeworn look. The huge, gilded mirror hanging near the dining table was only ten dollars, but when purchased, it was just a frame with no glass, and all the pretty decorative pieces were detached—the seller had them stored in a plastic bag. It probably comes as no surprise that Chris said "Why not?" and glued all the pieces back on. One more instance: the upper kitchen cabinets were originally shallower than Chris wanted, but he loved them, so he added more wood to the back to extend them.

We don't want to paint too rosy a picture: it's true that working with older materials can (and usually does) involve more time and effort—sometimes even blood, sweat, and tears. A lot of the projects Chris takes on are what we'd call next-level, varsity salvaging, and not everyone has the time, patience, or mad inspiration. But we find that keeping a creative "What if?" and "Why not?" attitude toward objects you see at the antique fair or projects in your space can lead to some pretty great discoveries.

Unwieldy piles of books flank a doorway, decorated with antique corbels found by the owner.

Q + A WITH CHRIS

Q: HOW WOULD YOU DESCRIBE YOUR DESIGN PHILOSOPHY?

A: I consider myself to be a designer-contractor, and I also do some decorating work. My philosophy is to make the spaces I work in more historically correct, to create a room that just looks like it was always that way, from the paint colors to the light fixtures. I'm focused on uncovering remnants of the original beauty of old houses, and then being really eclectic in the newer details and objects we bring in. I want to encourage people not to rely so much on the big-box hardware stores. I hope the spaces I design are really grown-up and elegant, but also funky and original. I'm a homebody, so I love having cool stuff around me, and I find that most people really do, too.

Q: WHY DID YOU CHOOSE DETROIT, AND THIS HOUSE IN PARTICULAR?

A: I first got into antiques living in the Hudson Valley, New York. I was actually born in Detroit, but that's not why I ultimately chose to come back here—I felt this was the place that I was needed the most, and I've found that people here have responded really positively to me and my work, which is really flattering.

But even putting all that aside, and even though it took a ton of work, this house is just one of the nicest spaces that I've lived in. I love the view of the Ambassador Bridge, and the windows on all sides of the house—when it's snowing, you feel like you're in a snow globe. I love my garden and my kitchen—I've cooked some wonderful dinners here.

Q: WHAT ARE SOME OF YOUR FAVORITE THINGS IN THIS SPACE?

A: One of my absolute favorite pieces is the hutch made of dark-stained beadboard by the dining table. I love that it's not too much or anything fancy—it looks like it was handmade. It almost feels too country to have in a city house, but I think that mix of time periods and styles really makes the room work. I just have a thing for beadboard, which is why I love the beadboard cabinet under the sink in the kitchen as well.

I'm also in love with the crazy, standalone, light-up ashtray in the living room. I got it from an antique dealer. I don't even smoke, but I just had to have it.

Q: WHAT WAS THE HARDEST THING ABOUT RENOVATING THE HOUSE?

A: This house was in such bad shape, with its weird layout—we had to tear everything down to the studs, jack it up because it was sinking, and reframe the whole thing. There were no windows, so the house was boarded up and dark for a long time, and in the winter it would be freezing. It took about five years to get from that to how you see the house now. Quite frankly, I probably wouldn't have taken it if it weren't for the location, the double lot with the garden, and the view of the Ambassador Bridge. People thought I was crazy, but the view kept me going.

In older spaces, it can feel like the projects never end. You have to get used to living in the middle of a ton of things going on, and knowing that your house is always going to be a work in progress.

LIGHTING

In an earlier section (page 82), we talked about natural light. Now we're going to focus on the artificial kind, and there are so many beautiful, unique examples of it in this book.

A good place to start when choosing lighting is to consider whether you're looking for something practical or something to set the mood. (Many great lights work both ways, of course.) Ask yourself a few questions: Will you read by this light? Are you going to be chopping onions under it? Or is it more important for the lighting in your space to be vibey and atmospheric, for lingering over cocktails long after dinner?

Lighting offers a fun chance to introduce a new era or material into a room: an Art Deco fixture can look great in a Mid-century Modern space, or industrial lighting can add a little grit and texture to a more polished home.

Your house might be blessed with killer original light fixtures. Or maybe you want to ball out on an awesome designer pendant—in the grand scheme of home renovation, lighting can be a relatively affordable splurge. That goes for the world of antiquing as well—you should definitely look up when you're out picking. With so many cool vintage light fixtures out there, we're not sure there's ever a good reason to stick with a regular old can light.

ABOVE: Dust-covered light fixtures in the Woodward Throwbacks warehouse waiting to find their next home.

OPPOSITE: The geometric silhouette of a pendant light by artist Isamu Noguchi is a dramatic and unexpected addition to the original features of the Dreamy House.

This Danish postmodern fixture is both a statement piece and a functional lamp that's bright enough to light up an entire kitchen.

An Art Deco light fixture salvaged from a demolished Detroit school.

Lighting can be a sculptural art object as well as a functional appliance that illuminates a room.

These antique pendant lights, which have an almost Moroccan vibe, are a great example of how a light source can be a different style than the rest of a room, but still fit in perfectly.

An industrial-style lamp pairs great with the old signage that serves as art at the Home Base.

FUNKY

FUNKY MEANS NO RULES. It's mixing textures, colors, and materials. It's retro and proud. It's leaning so hard into clutter it becomes art. It's hard to do well, but the houses we feature here have done it with flying colors. It's as if the full personality of the owners is expressed in all these homes with no filter—mind, body, and soul. We're tempted to say funky homes are so original, so unique to the people who live in them, that they're trendless. But we've noticed maximalism popping up more and more over the last few years, and we're not upset about it. Even if maximalism is becoming on trend, every funky space will be unique—because if it's filled and decorated with stuff you love, only you could have created it.

THE NOT YOUR GRANDMA'S HOUSE

The owner of this house describes her style as "grandma chic," and you'll totally get where she's coming from when you see the space. As you'd expect, many of the objects here are heirlooms and hand-me-downs—from owner Emily's grandmother and other relatives—all selected and incorporated into her own home with the confidence of someone with a fully developed personal style. But all that said, we've never seen any grandma's home that was quite like this. That's why we decided to call it the Not Your Grandma's House.

The Bagley neighborhood is a ten-mile haul from downtown Detroit, one of those areas where it's hard to believe you're still within city limits as you're cruising up the highway. It's bordered on one side by Livernois Avenue, one of Detroit's main thoroughfares, often referred to as the Avenue of Fashion for all the locally owned shops and businesses there. The neat rows of little brick houses are a testament to the huge numbers of middle-class families who thrived in Detroit at the height of its success, and who still proudly live here today.

It's a little funny to think about Emily's retro jewelry box of a space in the context of all these well-kept bungalows, where many of the families have lived for forty-plus years—it's probably one of the funkiest homes we're featuring in the book.

But Emily is very much a part of her neighborhood, and we also think this colorful, distinctive, one-of-a-kind space couldn't be more Detroit.

FAVORITE MOMENTS

One of the first things Emily hopes people see when they walk into her house is the fabulous moment she created in her dining room by installing wallpaper

195

(made by Spoonflower) on the ceiling. It's one of a few genius design decisions in this house that we've never really seen done before. The monochrome green paint on the walls (Avocado by Behr) is very of the moment—this is actually one of a few head-to-toe green dining rooms in this book—but the funky, unexpected pops of color in the wallpaper on the ceiling make it totally unique.

A color story connects this room to the living room just through the archway: Splashes of pink start in the pattern of the wallpaper and are picked up in different moments in the art on the gallery wall and even in the glassware on the brass bar cart. In the living room, pink is the main event, with Infatuation by Behr coating the walls, but more intense patterns in the retro couch and in the awesome, bohemian curtains continue the conversation between these two colors. By slowly building out from the wallpaper and the couch, Emily has created the perfect atmosphere for her grandma-chic home.

The second moment we want to feature in this house was an awesome surprise. When Emily asked if we wanted to see the basement, we were a bit taken aback at first—design book–worthy basements are relatively rare. But when we saw this time-capsule gem, we were totally floored.

Despite all the goodness going on upstairs, Emily says this is where people like to hang out when they come over, and we can totally see why. Great wood paneling, the moody mirror-backed bar complete with a brass footrail, and a ton of great linoleum tile flooring all make this space one of our favorites in the home.

The only thing we can really say about a basement like this is that if you're lucky enough to have one, please don't immediately write it off as dated and in need of an update. Take a minute to imagine yourself having a cocktail here, or displaying your vintage glassware collection on the shelves behind the bar, and you might not be so keen to give this room a more "on trend" overhaul. Personally, we love everything that makes the room a time machine, from the linoleum floor to the paneled ceiling.

OPPOSITE: The Not Your Grandma's House's bold sense of color and pattern is on display even in this relatively utilitarian corner of the kitchen.

SNAG THE STYLE

The Not Your Grandma's House is 100 percent unique—the owner's personality is on display on every surface, from the walls to the furniture to the shelves. If you want to create a space that just feels like you, here are a few tips to get started.

LAYER IT ON

The secret to building up a maximalist space like this, where a million different colors, textures, styles, eras, and tchotchkes happily coexist, is layering.

and sophisticated color schemes help to make it all work—it's a delicate balance, but pinks and greens and oranges and browns repeated throughout the home keep it feeling cohesive rather than crowded.

It's important to note that making sure everything matches perfectly is not necessary for successful layering. Oftentimes, just by picking out stuff you love and putting it all in the same space, your own personal style will start to shine through and tie it all together. If it doesn't seem to click at first, pour more on. The room may just start to work.

FAKE IT TILL YOU MAKE IT

Emily is a next-level antiquer, which means she's not afraid to put in a little elbow grease to make her vintage finds shine. Some of the objects here are textbook cases of upcycling, the classic technique of taking something that someone else might think of as trash and turning it into treasure—like the dresser she found on the curb and refinished, or the patio furniture she's currently using as the dining table.

One of our favorite examples of Emily's knack for creative reuse is the funky brass light fixture in the dining room, which looks like an expensive, atomic-era antique. This isn't a DIY arts-and-crafts book, but here's one fun idea: Emily's ceiling light is actually an old IKEA lamp that she paid six dollars for at a discount resale store. It was originally covered with paper flowers, but she took those off and spray-painted the lamp to look like brass.

The Not Your Grandma's House is proof that with a little creativity, you can find inexpensive ways to make your vision a reality. Investing in heirloom-level pieces is great, but so is using some DIY magic to turn something cheap into a future heirloom.

Emily says most of the rooms in the house started with one key element—the couch in the living room, or the wallpaper on the dining room ceiling—and she just piled on more stuff that she loves from there.

This applies to everything from covering seats with blankets, quilts, pillows, and cushions to creating multilevel vignettes of beloved knickknacks on tables and shelves. Contrasting textures look great next to one another throughout the house, from frilly lampshades and the rougher fabric of the couch to smoother glass, metal, and plastic. Bold

OPPOSITE: In the guest bedroom, the owner repurposed a plexiglass room divider to supplement the headboard.

LEFT: Texture, texture, texture. Fabric, pattern, metals, and foliage layer in the living room.

The living room in the Not Your Grandma's House narrowly avoids sensory overload by sticking to a mostly pink color palette.

The hidden basement bar in the Not Your Grandma's House is an absolute treasure.

Q + A WITH EMILY

Q: HOW DID YOU GET INTO VINTAGE AND ANTIQUES?

A: My grandmother has always been into old things, but my mom wasn't—she spent my entire childhood refusing to love thrift stores and antique malls. I still managed to get the bug for discovering hidden gems and things collecting dust on the racks and shelves, though—my room at my parents' house looked a lot like this house—just tchotchkes and stuff everywhere.

The funny thing is that when I purchased this house, my mom all of the sudden dove headfirst into thrifting. About half of the cool pieces here were found by her, and she's now thrifting and antiquing more than I am.

Q: WHAT'S YOUR PROCESS WHEN IT COMES TO DECORATING?

A: When you've been collecting for a while, you start to realize you can build whole rooms around your favorite pieces. I get an idea of where I'd like a favorite object to go, or think of something that I don't have yet that would complete my vision for a room, and go out and look for it. After that initial inspiration, it's a process of layering—starting small and building by adding more and more pieces. I switch things up constantly, so nothing is set in stone—if you came back in a few months, a gallery wall or shelf might look totally different. It's all a process of trial and error until I get a room to look right.

It also helps to have themes for rooms or color schemes to tie everything together. For example, I have a thing for Western stuff, so my guest room has a seventies cowgirl kind of vibe. Or knowing I want to build in more oranges or pinks or greens can help me decide what should go in a room.

Q: CARE TO SHARE ANY ANTIQUING TIPS?

A: My first tip is to make sure you're well-fed and hydrated, and that you've had your caffeine. If I'm shopping, I know I'm going to be there at least four hours, and I want to be focused on what's around me. Once you're there, you really have to scan, because there's so much stuff in some of these stores—like hundreds of things in one booth. I'll just stand there with my coffee and look. Sometimes I even go around again after I've been through one time, and I see totally new things.

Also, don't be afraid to dig. I've found some of my favorite things by really getting in there and rifling through the piles.

Last, don't be discouraged if you don't find something that appeals to you every time you go shopping—no one says you have to buy anything. Most of the time when I get something just because I feel like I should, it's not exactly what I wanted, and I regret it later. Trust me, there is so much stuff out there—if you take your time, you'll eventually find the perfect thing.

Q: WHAT'S ONE OF YOUR FAVORITE OBJECTS IN YOUR HOUSE?

A: It's so hard to choose—it's like choosing a favorite kid. I truly love everything in here. But one of the coolest things that I have is this mid-century tableside salad serving set with everything included—bowls, serving utensils, even salt and pepper shakers. It's meant to stand next to the table by itself. I can't wait to have people over and toss a salad tableside for my guests! I think I love it so much because I've just never seen anything else like it before.

FABRICS AND TEXTILES

Hopefully by now you know just how obsessed we are with texture—the crackly appeal of old wood, or the patinas that form on salvaged metal. But if your space is newer and didn't come with a lot of built-in texture, or you're not quite ready to go all in on a rustic piece of furniture made from reclaimed materials, luckily there's an easier and softer way to add texture to your space: fabrics and textiles.

Piling on pillows, quilts, rugs, and throw blankets, or mixing fabrics in your furniture, from brocade to leather, is a great opportunity to play with color, pattern, and feel—particularly if the textiles in question are vintage. Because these elements are portable and layer-able, rather than architectural, they're a great way to play with maximalism and clashing hues and styles. It's also possible to design a whole room around a specific textile, like a couch with a killer fabric or a rug with an eye-catching pattern.

We love fabrics and textiles most when they add an element of the unexpected—a Southwestern-style throw in a Victorian space, or layers and layers of quilts piled in an otherwise minimalist bedroom. A velvet couch might provide just the right contrast in a relatively industrial space. And the best part is, textiles are usually very portable. If a rug or pillow doesn't work in one room, it might just look perfect somewhere else.

ABOVE: The owner of the Not Your Grandma's House repurposed outdoor furniture for a dining set; the smooth plastic seats add yet another unexpected texture.

OPPOSITE: The velvet couch in the Home Base adds great atmosphere and texture to the living room.

A yellow gingham chair looks chic with a Southwestern-inspired pillow and the monochrome green walls of the Cosmopolitan House.

In the Not Your Grandma's house, every pillow is a chance to introduce a new tactile sensation.

Plush cushions soften the industrial gas canisters that have been repurposed as seating in the Garage House.

Leather dining chairs add another natural material to the Dreamy House, already characterized by tons of wood, plants, and stone.

Instead of a textile, beads substitute for curtains in the Not Your Grandma's House.

THE MOSAIC HOUSE

This light and airy space is tucked away in a delightful, labyrinthine compound in Hamtramck—a beloved city within Detroit, home to the Woodward Throwbacks warehouse as well as great international eats and dive bars galore. Owners Henry and Virginia have dreamed of opening a community ceramics school since they were teenagers, and this property with a hundred-year-old brick storefront, huge side yard, and a few apartments in the back seemed absolutely perfect—except for the fact that they found it in pretty rough shape. A few years, a lot of labor, and a Kickstarter later, the Ceramics School opened out front, and the lovely, tile- and pottery-filled apartment we're calling the Mosaic House was complete.

Finding your way to this space—through the shop and yard filled with kilns and pottery shards and dogs, and up some stairs—makes you feel like you've discovered a hidden oasis. This is exactly how Henry and Virginia meant it to feel: they built it to house artists in residence who come to work and study at the school, so it was important to them that the space feel homey, inspiring, and serene.

Much like the playful mosaics that decorate this space, which were handmade with leftover tiles the owners found on Facebook Marketplace, the process of designing this home was collaborative, creative, and improvisational. Like the resourceful artists they are, Henry and Virginia made do with things they had on hand, found online, or were given by friends to make a beautiful and cohesive retreat.

FAVORITE MOMENTS

Let's start in the kitchen, where a bunch of disparate elements come together to create a beautiful whole—kind of like the way a mosaic is made. There are tons of great salvage moments here. The countertops are made with narrow slabs of marble remnants placed side by side so all of the gorgeous, distinct colors and grains can play off one another. On the other side of the kitchen, thick chunks of wood that look exactly like butcher blocks are actually made from old bowling lanes.

But of course, the star here is the gorgeous mosaic backsplash, which Virginia painstakingly pieced together. The process went something like this: she put on safety goggles, threw tiles in a Tupperware, smashed them to pieces with a hammer, and then fit them all back together. The colors here work great: pale pastel pinks and purple grays in the mosaic bring out the natural pinks and grays in the marble, complemented by lovely mint-green paint on the cabinets. The cherries on top are the ridiculously cute ceramic knobs in the shape of animal faces that were—you guessed it—handmade by Virginia. Altogether it's a space that's simultaneously a working kitchen, a showcase for pottery and ceramic art the owners have collected, and a source of inspiration for any artist who spends time here.

There's another beautiful mosaic in the bathroom, which is our second favorite moment in the house. This work of art was even more labor intensive than the mosaic in the kitchen: in addition to going through the same process of breaking up old tile and fitting it together, Virginia also handpainted images of flowers, fruits, and animals on a bunch of the pieces. Thoughtful, personal details put this mosaic shower over the top, like the handmade planter and soap dish built into the walls, which add fun, function, and dimensionality to the space. Who wouldn't want to take a shower here?

SNAG THE STYLE

The Mosaic House is a member of a very elite group of houses within this book, in that nothing in it was bought new: everything was either found, salvaged, or purchased secondhand.

OLD-TILE STYLE

We're guessing most of you don't have a kiln right downstairs where you can fire up unique creations to decorate your space. But that's okay, because it's not like Henry and Virginia made every tile in the Mosaic House by hand. They made use of one of the home improvement industry's best-kept secrets: all of the extra pallets of tile you can find

Ceramics are as useful as they are beautiful, whether it's a collection of handmade vessels and tableware or a tile that doubles as a planter in the shower.

through online sources or practically anywhere that sells flooring.

You've probably heard of new old stock—bonus of materials that didn't quite get used up in a renovation project. Well, this is a prime example of how to use it. You can get small quantities of old tile for super cheap, and figuring out how to use it in your space encourages you to get creative. The beautiful mix-and-match ceramics in the Mosaic House certainly prove that perfectly pristine tile can be a bit overrated.

One last thing: just because Henry and Virginia are ceramicists doesn't mean they already knew how to install tile when they started renovating their space. Their secret? YouTube, which is honestly a great resource for all things home improvement. A small tile installation can be a great first DIY project, and a couple of videos on YouTube can really give you enough know-how to get started.

PLAYFUL AND PERSONAL

Attention to detail is just one of the things that makes the Mosaic House so special: the apartment is full of tiny, playful, incredibly personal design decisions. From the tiles hand-painted with little cobalt scenes, to adorable handmade ceramic cabinet pulls in the shape of animal faces, to the pottery and art gathered from students and friends covering practically every surface, Henry and Virginia have made this space reflect their passions and personalities.

Sometimes home design just gets too damn serious. If the funky houses in this book encourage you to do anything, we hope they give you permission to let pretentiousness go and commit 100 percent to what you love. Get those funky knobs for your kitchen cabinets. Turn the crayon art your niece made for you into a museum-level piece for your gallery wall. Proudly display your collection of Kewpie dolls on the shelf. This house demonstrates that playful and personalized can also be beautiful and sophisticated.

Q + A WITH HENRY + VIRGINIA

Q: WHAT DID YOU LEARN FROM RENOVATING THIS SPACE?

A: The renovation had to happen over time; we did it in phases as we could save up the money, and learned the skills we needed as we went. We also had a lot of help from friends and family members—it's huge to know people with reno expertise who are willing to lend a hand. That demolition phase is the hardest for us—when everything is messy and all over the place, it can be difficult to see the final vision.

In the end, renovating a house is definitely a lot of work, but it feels like a privilege. Not everybody gets the chance to make their space into exactly what they want.

Q: HOW DID YOU APPROACH DESIGNING THIS SPACE AS A COUPLE? WHAT DID EACH OF YOU BRING TO THE PROCESS?

A: Virginia is really good at the beginning stages, thinking about the layout and colors to create a vision of what the space will look like. She'll make sketches and fill them in with watercolor or colored pencil while the design is being refined. Henry tends to build by keeping almost everything—he can see a future in things and likes to hold on to them for future use. It's surprising how often the things he saves turn out to be super useful later on. He has also really become an incredible builder through-out the process of renovating this space, doing the bulk of the carpentry and the trades work.

Ultimately, both of us have a say in every space, and nothing happens unless we're both happy with the idea and come to an agreement about it. Making sure there's some aesthetic joy for both of us is a back-and-forth process.

Q: WHAT DOES HOME MEAN TO YOU?

A: We worked on renovating the ceramics school and the artist residency before we started focus-ing on our own home, because having a vibrant community is really important to us. We've always wanted to make a space—for ourselves and for others—that feels really human, and celebrates life and togetherness. And when we think about our perfect home, it's about community, too—we just imagine having friends over for dinner. We're hosts at heart—we want to have a beautiful life with our friends.

Q: WHY DESIGN WITH REUSED AND SALVAGED MATERIALS?

A: As artists, we know that almost anything can be used again. A lot of artists turn found and trash objects into sculpture and other kinds of artwork, and we think it's so important to use stuff that already exists whenever possible rather than con-tributing to the production of new things. Even if the impact is small, it's meaningful.

TILE

When we think of tile, the first things that come to mind are the gorgeous tile mosaic floors that grace the entryways of many older Detroit homes. These works of art welcome you into a house, and speak to the time and care that the artisan took to lay down all those tiny pieces.

Installing tile can be labor-intensive, but as a flooring or wall covering, it offers an opportunity to play with materials, color, and texture in a way that wood or paint may not. It also lasts as a living testament to luxury, artistry, and workmanship—think about the Greek and Roman mosaics that can still be seen at architectural sites today.

But playing with tile doesn't have to be a lot of work. Even just a few special tiles left over from another project or found on Facebook Marketplace can become playful accents in a room, subtle additions to a floor or shower that make anyone who notices them smile.

Another thing we love about tile is that it can speak to place through the materials it's made from and where they were made. Here in Detroit, tiles from Pewabic Pottery are famous, but many towns have their own version of a special local tilemaker, and collecting the objects they make can be a lot of fun. Putting a little more effort into choosing your tile can make your house into a story about the history and heritage of where you live.

ABOVE: The original yellow tiles around the Fire House's fireplace have a ton of character.

OPPOSITE: Iridescent Zellige tiles—a type of tile made in Morocco—add luxury and texture to any home.

A known quantity in the design world for years now, Zellige tiles are one of our favorite ways to introduce texture and polish to a kitchen or bathroom.

Older and grander Detroit homes often have beautiful tiled entryways, each with unique patterns and colors.

Hand-painted details add a ton of personality to the shower in the Mosaic House.

Hung on the wall in the Garage House, these salvaged tiles from Pewabic Pottery—a historic ceramic studio in Detroit—are a true work of art.

The original tile in the Charming House bathroom is full of character.

THE GALLERY HOUSE

Inside this nineteenth-century brick house in the Airport Sub neighborhood (named for the nearby regional Coleman A. Young Airport), the rooms are so filled with art that when you walk in, the effect is of entering a kaleidoscope of colors, images, textures, and artistic styles. Talk about maximalism and layering: the owner of this house, Torya, reached what many people might consider a point of saturation when it comes to artwork and continued piling more on, until you can measure the wall space without art in inches, and frames lean against one another on the floor.

Taking it all in, you have to give props to Torya, who has spent years building up her collection, avidly attending garage and estate sales, and developing her intuitive eye for great art with passion, practice, and research. If ever a space reflected who lived there, this would be it: Torya's personality is on display all over the walls, and it's a beautiful sight to see.

FAVORITE MOMENTS

It's hard to decide where to look in the living room, where most of the art is on display. But if we had to pick a favorite corner, it's the one with the huge portrait of French musician Serge Gainsbourg by Detroit artist Desiree Kelly. The scale of the painting anchors the space, and the yellow lettering in the background provides a nice complement and contrast to the colors of other paintings nearby, the warm light of the giant Edison-style bulb lamp in the foreground, and the happy plants that surround all the art.

The three-dimensional objects here are just as important as what's on the wall. We love the variety of furniture, from the Brutalist eighties side table made of plaster to the sexy leather lounger, to the butterfly sculpture, which belonged to Torya's mother. The trim surrounding the window, salvaged from a house in Corktown, completes the scene.

225

Our other favorite moment is in the kitchen, where the gallery tour continues. Typically, people don't put artwork in their kitchens, but we look at this room and wonder why not. We love how paintings cover every surface even here, framing the retro-inspired turquoise fridge, the window above the sink, and the wall over the countertop oven. Beautiful and functional ceramics and a happy wall of houseplants become their own kind of art in the context of all the paintings here. We spend so much of our time in the kitchen—there's no reason it should be simply utilitarian. In the Gallery House, Torya can contemplate a favorite piece of art while waiting for the kettle to boil.

SNAG THE STYLE

Even if you don't want to cover every available inch of your walls with art, there's a lot to learn from the Gallery House. (And who knows—you might find yourself changing your tune and filling up your walls as your art collection grows.)

DEVELOP YOUR EYE

When Torya walks you through her house, you feel like you're being given a personal tour of a museum. Torya has a near-encyclopedic knowledge of the pieces in her collection, from the Cy Twombly poster to the collage by artist Ray Johnson. But she isn't always drawn to a piece because she recognizes the artist or has an idea of when it might have been made. Usually, it's simply love at first sight; sometimes it's only later that she does some research to learn about dates, influences, periods, and provenances.

By constantly attending estate and garage sales and trawling Facebook Marketplace, Torya has definitely developed a signature style. Walking around her space, you can start to see some of her interests as a collector—abstracts and portraits, particularly of Black subjects—but there's a huge variety here, and that just reflects Torya following

her intuition. The idea of building a collection of this scale might seem intimidating at first, but the Gallery House is proof that you don't necessarily need formal training or any special expertise to get into art—you just need to have the interest and confidence in your own taste.

Local estate sales, garage sales, and Facebook Marketplace are great places get your collection started—and not only because these are great places to get a good deal. Regularly attending local sales will expose you to the kinds of art that are out there, help you fine-tune what you like, and key you in to local artists whose work may never have traveled far from the town or city where you live. We find that keeping your artistic investigations close

A gallery wall in the Gallery House. Portrait of Serge Gainsbourg by Detroit artist Desiree Kelly; additional artwork includes prints by Miró and Cy Twombly.

In the Gallery House, art covers every surface, even in the kitchen.

to home can be really rewarding; it often gives you a new perspective on local history, and having some pieces by local artists makes your collection specific and unique.

One last note: prints and posters are great pieces for novice collectors. These reproductions are often a lot cheaper than originals, but can be just as special.

GALLERY WALL 101

Torya's entire space is essentially a gallery wall, so this seems like a natural time to talk about building one. Here are some things to think about if you're inspired by the gallery walls in this house.

Number one: Scale. If you have pieces that are a variety of sizes, the larger ones are going to draw the most attention. It can be helpful to use larger art as a starting point, or an anchor, and build up organically around it.

Number two: As your collection grows, don't be afraid to go high and low. Sure, it makes sense to start at eye level, but in the Gallery House there are frames from floor to ceiling. Art hung at less conventional heights or in unexpected corners can catch your eye and make your gaze linger.

Number three: The 3D objects you put in the foreground are also important. In Torya's space, sculptures sit on tables and hang from the ceiling, plants obscure and showcase the art behind them, and the right lighting sets the mood. Coordinating your wall of art with the rest of the room takes it to the next level.

A few things you don't really see in the Gallery House: the spacing between the art isn't per-fectly even, and there isn't exactly a central color scheme that ties it all together. Making sure the gaps between each frame are relatively equal and selecting art with one dominant color are tips you often get for building a gallery wall, and if they work for you, that's great! But we think the perfectly imperfect look of Torya's art is pretty rad, too.

Our favorite corner in the Gallery House.

Q + A WITH TORYA

Q: WHAT GOT YOU INTO COLLECTING ART?

A: I started out collecting film posters. My father was really into movies, so when I was young, we used to go to the main branch of the Detroit Public Library on Saturdays and rent the weirdest films we could find. Then, when I was about seventeen, I saw a rare poster for the Fellini film *8½*, and for some reason I just really wanted to own it. It made me feel a certain way. I think my dad turning me on to watching films that most other kids my age weren't into at the time made me aware of art in a way. That gave me the bug and started me collecting.

Q: ANY TIPS FOR FINDING GREAT ART AT ESTATE SALES?

A: You have to know which sales to go to. This has been a part of my life so long that I've learned that if there's ever an estate sale at a house that was owned by an art teacher, I go. Or that when a storage company in Grosse Pointe is having a sale, there's bound to be some good stuff there, too. One of the best estate sales I ever went to was at the house of a guy who used to run estate sales—so of course he had some incredible art. When you get into the estate sale scene, you kind of just hear about ones that are happening, and have a sense of which are going to be good.

Q: TELL US ABOUT A FAVORITE PIECE IN YOUR COLLECTION.

A: The advertisement for Gitanes, a French brand of cigarettes, is cool. It's from the fifties, and it's what you call a giant poster—47 by 63 inches (which is really hard to frame). The size and the amazing colors definitely make it special. But what's even more interesting is that not only does it feature Black figures, but that they're two Black women, and they're smoking. Images like this from that time period are pretty rare.

Q: SO . . . WHAT ARE YOU GOING TO DO WHEN YOU RUN OUT OF ROOM FOR MORE ART?

A: I'll make it work. Come on! I know you can't keep everything, but you can keep the art. Always keep the art.

ART

Maybe more than anything else that you put in your space, art is a direct means of expressing your personality. When you start collecting art, you have unlimited choices—paintings, drawings, photographs, and prints available at antique stores, estate sales, local shops, and online, from artists long dead to contemporary ones producing more beautiful work every day. And every choice you make is a chance to say something about who you are.

It's fun to learn about artists, movements, styles, and everything that comes with them—from the story of how and why something was made, to where a piece came from and where it has been, to how much it might be worth. But really, selecting art for your home doesn't have to be complicated and requires no expertise—beyond following your heart and instincts, there truly are no rules. Art doesn't have to be fancy: we've even fallen in love with paint-by-numbers.

When it comes to displaying art in your space, it doesn't matter if dozens of tiny frames dot your walls, one huge piece takes up 50 percent of a room, or paintings lean against one another on the floor. Art in a hundred different styles and clashing colors can coexist with thoughtful arrangement and curation. An investment piece can look great next to a cheap but beloved film poster you've kept since high school.

If the art piece works, we don't question it. We just stand back, appreciate it, and ask, "Where'd you get that?" And usually, in response, we get a pretty good story.

ABOVE: An unconventional portrait looks striking against the exposed brick of the Forge House.

OPPOSITE: The beautiful floral mural in the Fire House was painted by the owner.

A great example of a mix-and-match gallery wall in the Not Your Grandma's House.

Think beyond prints and paintings; these cross-stiches in the Gallery House walk the line between folk art and pop art.

Favorite pieces in the Home Base: these wood-burned maps of the Upper and Lower Peninsulas of Michigan were made by a student of Kyle's grandpa, who was a teacher.

A collection of antique photographs and objects creates a beautiful gallery wall in the Charming House.

Art is a great way to show off things that are near and dear to your heart, like these posters for films made by the owner of the Raw and Refined House.

THE GALLERY HOUSE

THE FIRE HOUSE

In the world of Detroit real estate, the Land Bank—an organization formed around the time of the Great Recession to figure out what to do with all the vacant houses and lots in the city—is a big player. If you've ever heard stories about someone buying a falling-down house in Detroit for a thousand dollars, they probably purchased a Land Bank house.

There are a few conditions, of course. When you purchase a Land Bank home, you're buying it as is, and you need to occupy it yourself and bring it up to code within a set time frame, even if the house in question is in really rough shape—like, damaged in a fire, for example.

Maybe you've guessed by now that the home we're calling the Fire House—a Land Bank home a few miles northwest of downtown, not far from the famed mansions of Boston-Edison—is not a reclaimed former fire station (though that would be pretty cool, too). When the owner, Leah, found it, it had suffered extensive fire damage, enough that it was a total gut job—but a few precious original details remained. Leah made it her mission to save as much as possible, and then took things a step further: she decided to leave a lot of the fire damage the way she found it, putting a new perspective on all that crackle and smoke-stained goodness.

Leah's unique perspective on what deserves to be preserved hints at her broader approach to design, which is wonderfully creative and out of the box. Because the layout of the house was almost completely destroyed by the fire, she was free to rethink conventional home-reno dos and don'ts, and to make use of less traditional building materials. The result is a home that spotlights all the beautiful texture that comes from its history.

FAVORITE MOMENTS

The Fire House's large, open-format kitchen used to be the living room, which explains the fireplace with original yellow tiles. What could be a dark and gloomy room—with a black accent wall, dark trim,

239

Look more closely in the Fire House kitchen and you'll see black in a variety of textures, from fire-damaged ceiling planks to the tile backsplash to black plaster above the fireplace.

and partially preserved blackened ceiling boards—feels bright and airy thanks to wide salvaged French doors, large windows, white paint everywhere, and the shiny, white tiled floor. The textures of the new materials complement the texture of what was already in this room, from the beautifully grained plywood to the dramatic, almost smoky veins of the marble countertops.

You might need a second to get oriented in here, taking in the stove and sink next to the fireplace on one side of the room, and the fridge and L-shaped countertop on the other. The way the appliances are spread out, with all the roomy space in between, makes you realize that Leah has completely rethought the traditional kitchen layout. But the room undeniably works, both as a functional kitchen and a beautiful space in which to drink your morning coffee.

For our next favorite moment, we're going to zoom in on two details upstairs that were left over from the fire that almost destroyed this house. On the second floor, two crackled, fire-damaged doors stand side by side. Up close, the patinas here look like starbursts, or worn old leather. And in the bathroom, subway tiles were cracked by intense heat, leaving behind the most incredible patterns and crazing. We've never seen anything quite like these tiles before; the lines left behind by the fire could be woodgrain, or even fingerprints. We think the fact that Leah didn't see all this texture as something to be fixed is incredibly beautiful.

SNAG THE STYLE

Taking inspiration from this house might just change your concept of what a beautiful home looks like.

LET IT BE

The most obvious thing that the Fire House does differently from more traditional spaces is preserving the wear and tear that shows what this

Heat turned the subway tiles in the Fire House bathroom into works of art with one-of-a-kind patterns and textures.

home has been through. It's really even more than that: not only does Leah let the fire damage in her home be, she allows it to shine. Chips and cracks show in paint and wood finishes, ceiling beams are exposed, and the grain and pattern of the unpainted plywood cabinets look amazing.

Taking a page out of the Fire House's book means changing the way you see your space: you no longer automatically think that something old-looking or damaged is a problem to solve or a mess to clean up. Could the rough texture of that old door be beautiful? Does the chipped paint on the trim tell a valuable story? Might those dated tiles in your bathroom actually be an asset?

The bright and airy kitchen in the Fire House is completely DIY, including the beautiful mural by the fridge, painted by the owner.

Of course, there are some signs of wear and tear that are genuinely an issue and need maintenance for the sake of cleanliness or safety. But we think there's a lot to be said for retaining some of your home's original character, even if—especially if—it's not perfect. The Fire House's unique approach to preservation is sustainable, purposeful, and just plain cool.

PLYWOOD IS PRETTY

Plywood gets a bad rap; generally, it's viewed only as a cheaper alternative to hardwood, something to build with but not a finished product. Made of layers of wood veneer that have been glued together, plywood is indeed cheaper than other kinds of wood, but it's also strong, stable, and pretty easy to work with. There are tons of different kinds, from inexpensive plywood that's great for projects like roofing and subfloors, to the beautiful aspen plywood used for Leah's kitchen cabinets. Modern, refined, almost Scandinavian, plywood is the perfect complement to all the texture and older materials in Leah's space. It's pretty enough to remind us to incorporate plywood more often into our interior design.

Q + A WITH LEAH

Q: WHAT MADE YOU CHOOSE THE MATERIALS WHEN YOU WERE RENOVATING THIS SPACE?

A: Despite all the fire damage, I thought this house had a really distinct feeling, and I tried to honor that in all the design choices I've made. The salvaged French doors fit perfectly in this space, which made me feel like they were meant to be there. The marble countertops are new, but I picked that stone out specifically because I thought it matched that original feeling of the home.

Beyond that, sticking to one color scheme can help you make design decisions and visualize a space. There are a lot of blues and greens throughout the house, and I think that makes it feel consistent as you move from room to room.

Q: HOW WOULD YOU DESCRIBE YOUR RENOVATION AND DECORATING PROCESS?

A: First, I tried to use what was already in the space as much as possible. I'm a big fan of making do with what you have when it comes to design in general; a lot of the furniture and objects here were given to me, reclaimed from other houses nearby, or found on the side of the road. Even though the house was a total rehab, there was a lot of stuff that I ended up being able to make use of in the final design. Not only is reusing efficient, it also feels uniquely Detroit, as most of the structures and houses here were built in the 1920s, when they were using the choicest materials and everything was made to last.

Q: TELL US ABOUT ONE ESPECIALLY MEMORABLE DIY PROJECT IN THIS SPACE.

A: The stained-glass window by the stairs was a good one. I was able to restore one window in the house, but most of them were too charred and burnt out to be saved. To add some color to this window, I found the panes of stained glass at Architectural Salvage Warehouse here in Detroit, and then put them in the old window frame myself. It took a lot of work to make them fit.

Q: IS IT HARD TO LIVE IN A SPACE YOU'RE ALSO RENOVATING?

A: A renovation is such a long, ongoing process, even more so when you're living in the space and seeing it every day and trying to do everything yourself. But even once the renovation's "over," as a creative person, I think I'll still be getting ideas and wanting to try them out in my space. That means the process of renovating your home never really ends, and I think I'm okay with that.

OPPOSITE: Installing a salvaged stained-glass window was a favorite DIY project for the Fire House's owner.

TEXTURE

If we had to sum up Woodward Throwbacks in one word, it would probably be *texture*.

Texture has soul. It's something you just can't fake, and that's what we love about it. It makes things authentic, unique, impossible to replicate. Something with texture has had a life, and tells that life story right on its surface. Texture is about letting go and allowing nature to take its course. The impact time has on a material can't really be controlled, leading to bespoke colors, patterns, patinas, and sensations that are often their own works of art. Fire damage can make a piece of wood look like a fingerprint, or a tile like woodgrain; chipped paint can look like abstract art. No matter an object's history, the effect of texture is one of a kind, and there's value in things that can't be duplicated.

Admittedly, texture isn't for everyone. Textured things aren't polished; they can even be a little gnarly. But that doesn't mean something textured can't have clean lines, or fit into a bright, modernist home. Incorporating texture into modern design is one of our favorite challenges, and kind of sums up everything we do, from furniture to design.

We want to challenge people who see texture and just think old, damaged, or dirty to open their minds and look a bit closer. Maybe after reading this book, you'll start to rethink perfection, and whether something even needs to be perfect at all. We hope you'll start to look at your old house or furniture and imagine what it might be like to love what's already there—warps, chips, stains, nail holes, and all. Fixing up or restoring might bring value—what are you losing by ripping something out and throwing it away?

The modern construction and home improvement industries are incredibly wasteful. So much is lost when someone sees a little wear and tear and decides it means something needs to be thrown away and completely replaced. As the saying goes,

one person's trash is another's treasure—we've basically built a business on that. Making stuff out of scrap, leftovers, remnants, and waste not only encourages creativity but also builds that story into whatever you create. There's more interest in something made out of the unexpected, and we're all about design that makes your eyes linger so that you see something new every time you look. That's why the sustainability that comes from seeing the beauty in texture is just one of many benefits.

We like to think this concept of texture encapsulates what we do. It certainly sums up the beauty and complexity of Detroit, the city we love and owe it all to.

Original trim was gathered from all over the Renaissance House to showcase a bay window, with chips and cracked paint left to speak to the home's history.

Exposed brick is a quintessential element of many urban spaces. The different sizes, shapes, and colors are a classic example of texture in the home.

By pulling back layers of wallpaper, exposing the plaster, and leaving fragments of pattern, the owner of the Renaissance House used texture to unique effect.

Question your instinct to immediately refinish or replace wood floors with imperfections. We love the stories these chips and scratches tell.

We're obsessed with the patina caused by heat damage on the doors in the Fire House.

Priceless texture on the bench of a window seat in the Renaissance House.

MORE TIPS ON SECONDHAND SHOPPING

If you take anything from this book, we want it to be that there are no rules to great design made with reclaimed materials: it's all about getting out there, digging into the shelves at your local antique stores and garage sales, finding something you love, and running with it. We want your space to look like you, so telling you exactly where to go or what to buy would be the last thing on our minds.

That said, throughout the book, we tried to specify where a standout piece was picked up whenever possible, and made a point of name-dropping working artists in case you fall in love with their work and want to hit them up (we hope you do!). We mentioned a few brands and makers we come back to again and again. And we compiled this cheat sheet of how to get started with second-hand shopping. With these tools, we hope you'll go forth with confidence and inspiration. We can't wait to see what you create.

WHERE TO PICK

LOCAL STORES

Secondhand and resale shops, seemingly ubiquitous no matter where you live, are the obvious places to start. But you can get so used to these often-unassuming storefronts, sometimes found in anonymous strip malls, that it can take some practice to keep your eyes open to the wonders they can hold.

By local stores, we mean everything from antique shops and malls, to vintage and thrift stores, consignment and resale shops, even salvage yards. Each will sell different types of goods—from furniture to clothing and tchotchkes to old tiles and ornamental trim. But odds are you'll find some treasures no matter what, especially if you're willing to dig.

When in doubt, you can literally just open the map app on your phone, key in "antiques," and see what comes up. It's a fun thing to do with an open Saturday afternoon or even while you're traveling. Watch out—antiquing can become a habit real quick.

GARAGE AND ESTATE SALES

Making a great find at these less permanent resale events is more of a crapshoot, and takes willingness to pull over or go a bit off course when you see a sign on the side of the road. But being open to spontaneity can pay off—these are the places you can find some real deals, because the people running the sales are often very motivated to sell.

You can be a little more diligent about shopping garage and estate sales by looking them up online. Estate sales in particular tend to advertise in advance online, sometimes even with a preview of what will be on offer.

ANTIQUE FAIRS

At these annual or semiannual gatherings, vendors are bringing their best finds to one place. Don't necessarily expect to get bargains—antique sellers tend to schlep the special stuff to these events.

Search online to find antique fairs, or ask local picker friends or antique shop owners which are their favorites. Once you've made a weekend out of a trip to one of these festivals, you can officially consider yourself an antiquer.

DON'T FORGET THE INTERNET

Some of our favorite places to look are Facebook Marketplace, Chairish, 1stDibs, and eBay; you can even still find some good stuff on Craigslist these days. Chairish and 1stDibs tend to be more curated but also more expensive (try making a lowball offer); do be aware of potential scams on Facebook Marketplace.

Sure, you still have to put in the time when browsing the internet for thrifted finds, but at least you'll be doing it in your pajamas from your couch.

ACKNOWLEDGMENTS

You always hear the phrase "it takes a village," and it turns out that applies to many things—from building a business to writing a book. So there are a lot of people we've got to thank.

To our families—thank you for the support you have given us over the years. Time spent helping us accomplish our goals means so much to us.

To our friends, thank you for helping when we needed it. There have been a handful of times we have bribed you with free food and drinks in return for free labor. We are always so grateful to know you have our back.

To Megan, our writer, thank you for shaping our scrambled thoughts into a coherent message, and for steering us through the whole process of putting this book together.

To Jenna and Michelle, our photographers. We were so lucky to have you be a part of this project. Thank you for working around our schedules and really grinding out all these shoots.

To Eryn, our agent, for believing in us. When you approached us the last thing we had on our minds was writing a book. But from our first conversation we could really feel that you understood us and got what we were doing. It has been an amazing experience thus far and we can easily say we won't be here without you.

To Deanne and the rest of the team at Clarkson Potter: You all were amazing to work with.

To the Woodward Throwbacks staff—thank you for always putting up with our craziness. This last year we took on our biggest projects to date (some of which appear in this book, others still marinating). And you guys really killed it. A special thanks to our assistant, Angelica: You came on as a temporary employee for a shop project and never left. You probably had no idea what you were signing up for. But you were so much help on this book. It would have been hard to do it without you.

To all the homeowners whose houses appear on these pages. Thank you for letting us into your homes and trusting us to tell your stories. We're grateful to be able to show your homes through our eyes.

And last but not least, to Detroit—the neighborhoods, the streets, the architecture, the history, the people. This one was for you. You have always been our greatest inspiration. From the beginning, we made a point of creating this book entirely in Detroit: with a team of collaborators who are all based right here. We just love this city, and are so grateful to call it home.

Copyright © 2024 by Bo Shepherd and Kyle Dubay
Photographs copyright © 2024 by Gerard + Belevender

All rights reserved.
Published in the United States by Clarkson Potter/Publishers,
an imprint of the Crown Publishing Group, a division of
Penguin Random House LLC, New York.
ClarksonPotter.com

CLARKSON POTTER is a trademark and POTTER with
colophon is a registered trademark of Penguin Random
House LLC.

Library of Congress Cataloging-in-Publication Data is
available.

ISBN 978-0-593-58050-9
Ebook ISBN 978-0-593-58051-6

Printed in China

Editor: Deanne Katz
Designer: Jennifer K. Beal Davis
Art director: Mia Johnson
Production editor: Mark McCauslin
Production manager: Kelli Tokos
Compositors: Merri Ann Morrell and Zoe Tokushige
Copyeditor: Maureen Clark
Proofreader: Andrea Peabbles
Publicist: Natalie Yera
Marketer: Andrea Portanova

10 9 8 7 6 5 4 3 2 1

First Edition